Charles Finney
ON FAITH

Charles Finney
ON FAITH

CHARLES FINNEY

WHITAKER
HOUSE

CHARLES FINNEY ON FAITH
previously titled *The Secret of Faith*

ISBN: 0-88368-847-6
Printed in the United States of America
© 1999 by Whitaker House

Whitaker House
30 Hunt Valley Circle
New Kensington, PA 15068
visit our web site: www.whitakerhouse.com

Library of Congress Cataloging-in-Publication Data

Finney, Charles Grandison, 1792–1875.
  [Secret of faith]
  Charles Finney on faith / by Charles Finney.
    p.   cm.
Originally published: The secret of faith. New Kensington, PA: Whitaker House, © 1999.
  ISBN 0-88368-847-6 (pbk.)
  1. Faith. I. Title.
  BV4637 .F45 2002
  234'.23—dc21
                                        2002012141

1 2 3 4 5 6 7 8 9 10 11 12 / 10 09 08 07 06 05 04 03 02

Contents

Introduction

How can I have a right relationship with God? This question has been asked by mankind down through the centuries. In John 6, the people asked Jesus this same question, using different words: *"What shall we do, that we may work the works of God?"* (v. 28). Jesus' response was as follows: *"This is the work of God, that you believe in Him whom He sent"* (v. 29). Jesus' answer gives us the secret to a right relationship with God. The secret is faith.

Of course, once we have obtained this right standing with God, this justification through faith, the next questions we often ask are, How can I obtain sanctification—holiness in everyday living? How can I be consecrated—fully dedicated and devoted—to God? How can I rise above my sinful and worldly desires and behavior? The answer is the same: the secret is faith.

As we discover in this insightful book, the key is to place our faith in who Jesus is. He is our Redeemer; He is our Sanctifier; He is our Mighty God. Indeed, He is our All-sufficiency in all things. Even more than that, He lives within us so that we may please and honor God in all things.

Few are more qualified to address the vital topics of justification and sanctification than Charles Finney. His powerful preaching won thousands to Christ, and his inspiring books continue to reach thousands more. In this book, he presents a striking picture not only of the need for salvation in God, but also the necessity of a close, holy walk with God. Most importantly, Finney shows how these needs can be met through the secret of faith.

PART ONE

Victory over Sin

Then they said to Him, "What shall we do, that we may work the works of God?" Jesus answered and said to them, "This is the work of God, that you believe in Him whom He sent."
—John 6:28–29

Chapter 1

The Bondage of Trying to Work Your Way to Heaven

Many wrong answers are commonly given to the question, *"What shall we do, that we may work the works of God?"* (John 6:28).

If the question were asked of a Jew, he would answer, "Keep the law, both moral and ceremonial," that is, keep the commandments.

To the same question, some Christians would answer, "Do your best according to the light that you have, and you will obtain grace and be saved." But if the one asking the question is unrepentant and does not have faith, this answer amounts to the following: you must obtain grace for conversion by your unrepentant works; you must become holy by your hypocrisy; you must work out sanctification (holiness in everyday living) by sin.

No Christian would *officially* point someone to the law as the ground of justification, but nearly the entire church would give a reply to this question that would amount to the same thing. Their answer would be a law-oriented and not a Gospel-oriented answer. Any answer to this question that does not distinctly recognize faith as the foundation of all virtue in repentant sinners is a law-oriented answer.

We must tell the one who asks this question that faith is the first and fundamental duty. Without faith, all virtue, all giving up of sin, all acceptable obedience is impossible. Unless we make this clear, we are misdirecting the person. We lead him to believe that it is possible to please God without faith and that it is possible to obtain grace by works of law.

There are only two kinds of works—works of law and works of faith. Now, if a person does not have "the faith that works by love" (see Galatians 5:6), we must not set him on a course of works to get it. This is directing him to get faith by works of law! Whatever we say to him must clearly convey the truth that both justification and sanctification are by faith without works of law. Anything we say to the contrary is the law; it is not the Gospel.

Before an unbeliever has faith, he cannot possibly do anything but works of law. His first duty, therefore, is faith. Every attempt to obtain faith by unbelieving works is an attempt to lay works at the foundation and make grace a result. It is the direct opposite of gospel truth.

Facts that arise in everyday life show that what I have stated is the experience of almost everybody, both unbelievers and professing Christians. Whenever a sinner begins to earnestly debate the question, "What should I do to be saved?" he resolves, as his first duty, to break away from his sins, but he does so in unbelief. Of course his reformation is only outward. He determines to do better—to reform in this, that, and the other thing—and thus prepare himself to be converted. He does not expect to be saved without grace and faith, but he attempts to get grace by works of law.

The same is true of multitudes of anxious Christians who are asking what they should do to overcome the world, the flesh, and the devil. They overlook the fact that *this is the victory that has overcome the world, even our faith*" (1 John 5:4 NIV), that it is with *"the shield of faith"* (Ephesians 6:16) that they are *"to quench all the fiery darts of the wicked one"* (v. 16).

Anxious Christians ask, Why am I overcome by sin? Why can I not get above its power? Why am I the slave of my appetites and passions and the laughingstock of the devil? They look around for the cause of all this spiritual wretchedness and death. At one time, they think they have discovered it in the neglect of one duty, and, at another time, in the neglect of another duty. Sometimes they imagine they have found the cause in yielding to one sin, and sometimes in yielding to another. They put forth efforts in this direction and in that direction; they patch up their righteousness on one side while they make a tear in the other. They spend years running around in circles and making dams of sand across the current of their own corruptions. Instead of at once *"purifying their hearts by faith"* (Acts 15:9), they are busy trying to stop their hearts' bitter waters from overflowing.

Why do I sin? they ask. Looking around for the cause, they come to the "wise" conclusion, It is because I neglect such and such a duty—in other words, I sin because I do sin! They ask, But how can I get rid of sin? and they answer, By doing my duty. In other words, they are saying, I can get rid of sin by ceasing from sin!

Now, the real question is, Why do they neglect their duty? Why do they commit sin at all? Where is the foundation of all this evil? Perhaps you reply, The foundation of all this wickedness is in the corruption of our nature, in the wickedness of the heart, in the strength of our evil tendencies and habits. But all this only brings us back to the real question again: how are these sinful habits and this corrupt nature to be overcome? I answer, By faith alone. No works of law have the least tendency to overcome our sins. Rather, they strengthen the soul in self-righteousness and unbelief.

The great and fundamental sin, which is at the foundation of all other sin, is unbelief. The first thing is to give this up—to believe the Word of God. There is no breaking away from one sin without this. *"Whatever is not from faith is sin"* (Romans 14:23). *"Without faith it is impossible to please Him"* (Hebrews 11:6).

Perhaps you have noticed that when the backslider and the convicted Christian are agonizing to overcome sin, they will almost always go to works of law to obtain faith. They will fast, pray, read, struggle, and outwardly reform, and thus endeavor to obtain grace. Now, all this is in vain, and it is wrong. Are you asking, Shouldn't we fast, pray, read, and struggle? Should we sit down and do nothing? I answer, You must do all that God commands you to do, but begin where He tells you to begin. Furthermore, do it in the manner in which He commands you to do it, that is, by exercising "the faith that works by love." (See Galatians 5:6.) "Purify your heart by faith" (Acts 15:9). Believe in the Son of God. Furthermore,

Do not say in your heart, "Who will ascend into heaven?" (that is, to bring Christ down from above) or, "Who will descend into the abyss?" (that is, to bring Christ up from the dead). But what does it say? "The word is near you, in your mouth and in your heart" (that is, the word of faith which we preach). (Romans 10:6–8)

Now, these facts show that even under the Gospel, almost all who profess religion, while they reject the Jewish concept of justification by works of the law, have after all adopted a ruinous substitute for it; they suppose that in some way they are to obtain grace by their works.

I will discuss in the next chapter how one can step out of the bondage of works and into the freedom of faith.

Chapter 2

The Freedom of Faith

U nder the circumstances in which the question was asked, Christ gave the only proper answer to the question, *"What shall we do, that we may work the works of God?"* (John 6:28). His answer was, *"This is the work of God, that you believe in Him whom He sent"* (v. 29).

In order to understand the appropriateness of the answer, we must understand the meaning of the question. The context shows that the question was asked by certain unbelieving Jews. These Jews asked what they could do to work the works of God—in other words, to obtain the favor of God. Christ understood them as asking what works would be acceptable without faith. He therefore answered, *"This is the work of God, that you believe in Him whom He sent."* It was as if He was saying, "Nothing that you would recognize as a work of God is really a work of God."

Faith is the first great work of God, without which it is impossible to please Him (Hebrews 11:6). To a Jew, this answer would imply that he must believe Christ to be the Messiah foretold in the Scriptures. And to everyone, the answer implies not only a general confidence in the character of God, but trusting in His atonement and saving grace instead of trusting in works of law for justification.

Christ's answer is the only proper answer to be given to a person in a state of unbelief. I will show both what I do *not* mean by this statement and what I *do* mean by it.

What I Do Not Mean

I do not mean that there is no good work except faith. Nor do I mean that faith without works is acceptable to God. (See James 2:17.)

Nor do I mean that faith nullifies the law (see Romans 3:31) and sets aside the necessity of good works. James set the necessity of works, as the result of faith, in a strong light:

Thus also faith by itself, if it does not have works, is dead. But someone will say, "You have faith, and I have works." Show me your faith without your works, and I will show you my faith by my works. You believe that there is one God. You do well. Even the demons believe; and tremble! But do you want to know, O foolish man, that faith without works is dead? Was not Abraham our father justified by works when he offered Isaac his son on the altar? Do you see that faith was working together with his works, and by works faith was made perfect? And the Scripture was fulfilled which says, "Abraham believed God, and it was accounted to him for righteousness." And he was called the friend of God. You see then that a man is justified by works, and not by faith only. Likewise, was not Rahab the harlot also justified by works when she received the messengers and sent them out another way? For as the body without the spirit is dead, so faith without works is dead also.

(James 2:17–26)

Nor do I mean that there are no other directions that may be given to a seeking sinner or Christian that, if followed, would not amount to the same thing in the end as the directions in John 6:29. In one of my revival lectures, I said, "You may give the sinner any direction or tell him to do anything that includes a right heart." To repent, to submit, to give the heart to God, and all the other directions I gave in this lecture *imply* faith. If I were to give the same lecture again, I would give a greater emphasis to faith and show that the exercise of faith is the first thing to be done. It is upon the exercise of faith that repentance, submission, love, and every other grace depend.

What I Do Mean

Now, allow me to explain what I do mean when I say that Christ's answer—*"This is the work of God, that you believe in Him whom He sent"* (John 6:29)—is the only proper answer for a person in unbelief. I do mean that no works are good works, or are in any sense acceptable to God, unless they proceed from faith. Let it be forever remembered that *"without faith it is impossible to please Him"* (Hebrews 11:6) and *"whatever is not from faith is sin"* (Romans 14:23).

Christ's answer is the proper answer because both justification and sanctification are by faith alone. Romans 3:30 says, *"There is one God who will justify the circumcised by faith and the uncircumcised through faith."* And Romans 5:1 says, *"Therefore, having been justified by faith, we have peace with God through our Lord Jesus Christ."* Also, Romans 9:30–32 says,

> *What shall we say then? That Gentiles, who did not pursue righteousness, have attained to righteousness, even the righteousness of faith; but Israel, pursuing the law of righteousness, has not attained to the law of righteousness. Why? Because they did not seek it by faith, but as it were, by the works of the law.*

But perhaps you will not clearly see the truth of this unless I make a remark or two on the nature of faith.

The first element of saving faith is a realization of the truth of the Bible. But this alone is not saving faith, for Satan has this realization of truth, which makes him tremble (James 2:19).

A second element of saving faith is the consent of the heart or will to the truth perceived by the intellect. It is a sincere trust. It is resting the mind in those truths. Furthermore, it is a yielding up of the whole being to their influence.

Now, it is easy to see that without the consent of the will, there can be nothing but an outward obedience to God. Without confidence in her husband, a wife can do nothing more than outwardly perform her duty to him. It is a contradiction to say that she can perform her duty from the heart without confidence. The same is true in matters of parental authority and all other authority. We may perform works of law without faith—that is, we may serve out of fear or hope or some selfish consideration—but without faith, obedience from the heart is impossible. This faith operates by love (Galatians 5:6), and to say that we can obey from the heart without love is a contradiction of terms.

To seek faith by works of law is an utter abomination. It is as abominable as attempting to purchase the Holy Spirit with money. (See Acts 8:18–20.) It is setting aside God's testimony about our utter depravity and attempting to palm off our unbelieving, heartless works upon an infinitely holy God. It is an attempt to purchase God's favor instead of accepting grace as a sovereign gift.

It is as preposterous as it is wicked. It is seeking to please God by our sins—to purchase faith by making God a liar. (See 1 John 1:10.)

To give any answer other than Christ's answer to someone in unbelief—to tell him to perform any work with the expectation that by it he will obtain faith—is wrong. It strengthens him in self-righteousness. It prolongs his rebellion. Either it leads him to settle down in a self-righteous hope, or it produces, in the end, discouragement and blasphemy.

Repentance, love, submission, and every other holy activity both imply and proceed from faith. It is impossible to repent without having confidence in the character and requirements of God, for what is repentance but to wholeheartedly assent to God's righteousness and condemn ourselves? It is equally impossible to submit to God without confidence in Him and in His requirements. It is also impossible to love God without faith.

Christ's answer is the proper answer because all right affection and all good works will proceed from faith. Christ was not afraid of producing a "sit down and do nothing" spirit by putting so much emphasis on faith. He knew very well that true faith naturally produces every other inward grace and all outward good works.

Faith is the only thing that receives Christ with all His powerful, sanctifying influences into the heart. The Bible consistently shows us that the sanctified soul is under the influence of an indwelling Christ. Now, exercising faith is opening the door so that Christ can reign in the heart.

Who will pretend that any works are truly good unless they result from Christ's influence? Who will pretend that any true faith exists in the mind unless it results from Christ's influence in the mind?

Now, if all this is true, it is plain that the proper response to the question, *What shall we do, that we may work the works of God?* (John 6:28), is to receive Christ through faith. If this is done, all else will be done. If this is neglected, all else will be neglected.

In the next chapter, we will see in greater detail the victory that comes through faith.

Chapter 3

You Can Have Victory

❖━◆━◆━◆❖

In considering how to have victory over sin, we must turn again to our text: *"Then they said to Him, 'What shall we do, that we may work the works of God?' Jesus answered and said to them, 'This is the work of God, that you believe in Him whom He sent'"* (John 6:28–29).

As we have seen, it was to unbelieving Jews that Jesus answered, *"This is the work of God, that you believe in Him whom He sent."* Under other circumstances, another answer might have been given.

For example, in other circumstances, it might be important and proper to direct the careless, unawakened sinner, who knows nothing of his depravity or helplessness, to the law of God as the standard that it is his duty to follow. It is not that we expect to directly bring about holiness in him by doing this, but we expect to convict him of sin. For this reason, we find Christ requiring the young man who was wrapped up in self-righteousness to *"keep the commandments"* (Matthew 19:17). Christ was bringing before his mind his supreme love of the world. This produced regret and discouragement in the young man. When he was required to part with all that he had and follow Christ (Luke 18:22), he *"became very sorrowful"* (v. 23).

However, to the anxious sinner who asks, *"What shall [I] do, that [I] may work the works of God?"* (John 6:28), Christ's answer in our text is the only appropriate answer. Also, to the Christian who is seeking sanctification, this is the only appropriate answer. In short, to anyone who is convinced of his real character, this is the only proper answer.

But to the one who is already full of faith and love and the Holy Spirit, another answer may be given, simply because he means something different when he asks this question. When he asks, *"What shall [I] do, that [I] may work the works of God?"* his heart breaks forth with the question, "What should I do to honor and glorify God?"— not "What should I do to be saved?" Such a person should be directed to the whole instructional part of the Bible. "Do this" and "avoid that" are just the instructions that he needs. He will eagerly seize them so that he may glorify God with all his heart.

Such a person needs instruction, not orders and threats. The instructional part of the Bible is just what his circumstances and state of feelings demand. The commands of God's Word will not produce in him a legalistic spirit that will prove a stumbling block to his soul. He will not self-righteously perform the duties in the Bible. On the contrary, his *heart* will go forth to meet his responsibilities and to perform the requirements of God.

Valuable Truths about Overcoming Sin

We learn many valuable truths from our study of John 6:28–29. First of all, we come to understand Romans 9:30–32, which I quoted before:

> *What shall we say then? That Gentiles, who did not pursue righteousness, have attained to righteousness, even the righteousness of faith; but Israel, pursuing the law of righteousness, has not attained to the law of righteousness. Why? Because they did not seek it by faith, but as it were, by the works of the law.*

The Jews sought to please God by their actions. They tried to please God without faith. But all their righteousness was like filthy rags (Isaiah

64:6). Meanwhile, the Gentiles had lived in open rebellion. But when they heard the Gospel, they believed it at once, instead of turning to works of law. Exercising "the faith that works by love" (Galatians 5:6), they attained to *"the righteousness which is from God by faith"* (Philippians 3:9).

We learn another valuable truth from this study. We see why the people in the church are not living in holiness. They overlook the fact that faith alone can produce acceptable obedience to God. They try to obtain faith by works instead of first exercising the faith that will produce in them a clean heart. (See Acts 15:9.) In this way, they seek for sanctification in vain.

How common it is to see people full of bustle and works and outward efforts—fasting, praying, giving, doing, struggling—and after all that, they do not have the fruits of the Spirit: *"love, joy, peace, longsuffering, kindness, goodness, faithfulness, gentleness, self-control"* (Galatians 5:22–23). They have not, after all, *"crucified the flesh with its passions and* [lusts]" (v. 24.) They do not live in the Spirit and walk in the Spirit. (See verse 25.) They do not experience the truth of the saying, *"You will keep him in perfect peace, whose mind is stayed on You, because he trusts in You"* (Isaiah 26:3). Without this trust, they cannot have peace; they cannot be sanctified.

Others try to force themselves to exhibit the various Christian virtues—love, submission, and so on—without faith. They forget that repentance and submission—the surrendering of our wills to the will of God—are the results of faith. We certainly cannot submit to God without confidence in the character of God. In short, every Christian virtue has faith as its foundation.

We learn yet another important truth from our study of John 6:28–29. We see why the Bible puts so much emphasis on faith.

We also see what the problem is with those who are constantly complaining about religion. They seem to know that they are guilty, but they do not understand why they are guilty. Sometimes they think that a neglect of one duty is the problem, and other times the neglect of another duty. They determine to break away from this sin and that transgression, and practice this self-denial and that duty—all without the faith that fills the heart with love. As a result, they go around and around in circles. They do not see that unbelief is their great, their damning sin. If this sin is not removed, no other sin can be repented of or forgiven. All their efforts are entirely legalistic, hypocritical, and futile until they exercise faith.

Let us go to the other end of the spectrum. Some people set aside all biblical instruction and think that obedience to the commands of God is legalism. They are mistaken. They do not make the distinction that I am making. What I am saying is this: if people without faith, in an unsanctified state, determine to obey the commandments of God, their efforts will be legalistic, self-righteous, and disastrous. To them, the precepts of the Gospel, as well as the commandments of the law, are a horrible pit of quicksand.

If you throw a man into quicksand, the more he struggles, the deeper he sinks. So it is with the person who is struggling to obey God without faith. Every effort at obedience without faith is sin; and since it strengthens self-righteousness, it is sinking him further and further away from God and hope. The more fiercely he struggles, the more desperate and alarming his case becomes. The mud surrounds him, clings to him, suffocates and kills him. To an unbelieving heart, the commands of God are a snare and a pit. They are suffocating quicksand. Without faith, there is ruin and damnation in them.

Deliverance through Faith

We see how to the Jews, and to all unbelievers, the commandments of God are a stumbling block. All outward conformity to them is useless—yes, disastrous. Love without faith is impossible. Consequently, the merciful directions and teachings contained in the instructional parts of the Gospel are made the food of self-righteous-ness and the snare of death.

But to those whose souls are full of faith and love, the commandments of God are just the instruction they need when, in their igno-rance, they earnestly ask what they should do to glorify God. "Do this" and "avoid that" are just the things that hearts of love will seize. They are the needed directions of their heavenly Father.

Someone may ask, Do people not learn to exercise faith by what you call legalistic efforts and by trying to obey the law's directions? No. They learn only that all such directions are futile and that they are totally depraved and depen-dent, which they ought to have believed before. They determine to pray and read and struggle, expecting at every meeting they attend, and with every prayer they offer, to obtain grace and faith. But they never do until they are completely dis-couraged and despair of obtaining help in this way.

The story of every self-righteous sinner's con-version and every anxious Christian's sanctifica-tion would develop this truth—that deliverance did not come until they saw by experience that their self-righteous efforts were utterly futile and they abandoned them as useless and threw the whole matter on the sovereign mercy of God. Giving the matter to the sovereign mercy of God is the very act of faith that they should have put forth long before. But they would not do it until they had tried every other means in vain.

But perhaps you are saying, If by this self-righteous struggle they learn their depravity and dependence, and in this way come to prove the truth of God, why not encourage them to make these efforts as at least an indirect way of obtaining faith? I answer, Blasphemy and drunkenness, and any of the most shocking sins, may be, and often have been, the means of working conviction that has resulted in conversion. Why not encourage these things? The truth is, when a sinner's attention is awakened and he is convicted and asks the question, "What should I do?" and when a Christian, struggling with his remaining corruption, asks the same question, why should they be thrown into the horrible pit of which I have spoken? Why not tell them at once, *"This is the work of God, that you believe in Him whom He sent"* (John 6:29)?

Let me say something to you who would ask the question, *"What shall we do, that we may work the works of God?"* (v. 28). Don't wait to fast, read, pray, or to do anything else. Don't expect to break away from *any* sin in your unbelief. You may break away from the outward act—you may substitute praying for swearing, reading your Bible for reading unwholesome material, sobriety for drunkenness, honesty for theft, industry for idleness, and anything you please. But that is, after all, only exchanging one form of sin for another. It is only varying the *mode* of your warfare. Remember that in unbelief, whatever your conduct is, you are in rebellion against God. Faith would instantly sanctify your heart, sanctify all your actions, and render them, in Christ Jesus, acceptable to God. Unbelief is your great, heinous, damning sin—against which the heaviest thunderbolts of Jehovah are hurled.

Don't wait for any particular revelation of Christ before you believe. When people in the state of mind that I have been describing hear those who live in faith describe their revelations of Christ, they say, "Oh, if I had such revelations, I could believe. I must have these before I can believe." Now, you should understand that these revelations are the result of faith, not the cause of it. These revelations are what faith discovers in those passages of Scripture that describe Christ. Faith grasps the meaning of those passages. It sees in them the very things that you mistakenly expect to see before you exercise faith and that you think would produce faith. Take hold, then, of the simple promise of God. Take God at His word. Believe that He means just what He says. This will at once bring you into the state of mind that you are seeking.

A believer in New York asked me in a letter what she should do to obtain the blessing of sanctification. My dear child, you ask whether you will obtain sanctification by reading the Bible, by prayer, by fasting, or by all these put together. Now, let what I have said be your answer. Know that, in the absence of faith, none of these things will help you grow any better or find any relief. You speak of being in darkness and of being discouraged. No wonder you are, since you have plainly been seeking sanctification by works of law. You have *"stumbled at that stumbling stone"* (Romans 9:32). You are in the horrible pit of quicksand that I have spoken of. Exercise faith in the Son of God immediately. It is the first thing—the only thing—you can do to rest your feet upon the Rock, and it will immediately put a new song in your mouth. (See Psalm 40:2–3.)

PART TWO

——◄◆◆►——

Victory
over the World

For everyone born of God overcomes the world.
This is the victory that has overcome the world,
even our faith.
—1 John 5:4 NIV

Chapter 4

What Does It Mean to Overcome the World?

---❖❖❖---

In the pages that follow, I intend to answer four questions: What does it mean to overcome the world? Who overcomes the world? Why do they overcome? How do they overcome?

First, what does it mean to overcome the world? It means to get above the spirit of covetousness that possesses the people of the world. The spirit of the world is the spirit of covetousness. It is a greediness after the things of the world. Some worldly individuals covet one thing and some another, but all worldly men and women are living in the spirit of covetousness. This spirit has supreme possession of their minds.

Now, the first thing in overcoming the world is overcoming the spirit of covetousness. The person who has not risen above this spirit of bustling and scrambling after what this world offers has by no means overcome it.

Overcoming the world means not being engrossed in it. When a person has overcome the world, his thoughts are no longer engrossed in worldly things. A person certainly does not overcome the world unless he gets above being absorbed and swallowed up by its concerns.

Now, we all know how extremely engrossed worldly individuals are in some form of worldly pursuit. One is perhaps swallowed up by study, another by politics, a third by making money, and a fourth by fashion and pleasure. But each in his chosen way makes earthly concerns the all-engrossing purpose.

The person who wants to gain the victory over the world must overcome not only one form of its pursuits, but every form. He must overcome the world itself, along with all that it uses to allure the human heart.

Overcoming the world also implies overcoming the fear of the world. It is a sad fact that most people, and indeed all worldly people, have much regard for public opinion. They dare not follow their consciences when doing so would incur the frown of society. One man is afraid that his business would suffer if his course were to run counter to public opinion. Another man fears that standing up for the truth will injure his reputation. Oddly enough, he imagines that advocating an unpopular truth would diminish his good influence—as if a man could exert a good influence without maintaining the truth.

Great multitudes, it must be admitted, are under this influence of fearing the world. Yet some, perhaps many, are not aware of this fact. If they could thoroughly investigate the reasons for their backwardness in duty, they would find fear of the world among the foremost. Their fear of the world's displeasure is so much stronger than their fear of God's displeasure that they are completely enslaved by it.

Who does not know that some ministers dare not preach what they know is true, even if it is very important, lest they offend someone whose good opinion they are seeking? Perhaps the community where a certain minister lives has a weak economy, and the favor of some of its rich men seems indispensable to its very survival. Hence, the terror of these rich men is continually before the minister's eyes when he prepares a sermon or preaches or is called to take a stand in favor of any cause that may be unpopular with those who possess more wealth than piety. Oh, this bondage to man! So many gospel ministers are so troubled by it that their cowardly policy is virtually to renounce Christ and serve the world. Overcoming the world means to thoroughly subdue this slavery to men.

In addition, overcoming the world implies overcoming a state of worldly anxiety. You know that there is a state of great worry and anxiety that is common and almost universal among worldly individuals. This is perfectly natural if the heart is set on obtaining worldly good. Such a heart has not learned to receive all good from the hand of a great Father and to trust Him to give or withhold with His own unerring wisdom. But the one who loves the world is the enemy of God; he can never have this childlike trust in the Father, or the peace of soul that it imparts.

Therefore, worldly individuals are almost incessantly in a fever of anxiety lest their worldly schemes should fail. Sometimes they get momentary relief when everything seems to go well, but some mishap is sure to befall them at some point soon afterward. Scarcely a day passes that does not bring with it some gnawing anxiety. Such men are like *"the troubled sea, when it cannot rest, whose waters cast up mire and dirt"* (Isaiah 57:20). However, the man who gets above the world gets above this state of ceaseless and destructive anxiety.

There is a worldly spirit, and there is also a heavenly spirit. One or the other exists in the heart of every man and controls his whole being. Those who are under the control of the world have not, of course, overcome the world. No man overcomes the world until his heart is permeated with the spirit of heaven.

Victory over the world implies that we cease to be enslaved to the spirit of the world in any of its forms. One form that the spirit of the world assumes is being enslaved to the customs and fashions of the day. It is amazing to see what a goddess Fashion becomes. No heathen goddess was ever worshiped with costlier offerings or more devout homage. And surely no heathen deity since the world began has had more universal patronage. Where will you go to find the worldly man or woman who does not hasten to worship at Fashion's shrine? But overcoming the world implies that the spell of this goddess is broken.

Those who have overcome the world are no longer anxious either to secure its favor or to avert its frown. To them, the good or bad opinion of the world is a small matter. *"With me,"* said Paul, *"it is a very small thing that I should be judged…of man's judgment"* (1 Corinthians 4:3 KJV). This is true of every real Christian. His concern is to secure the approval of God; his chief interest is to commend himself to God and to his own conscience. (See Acts 24:16.) No man has overcome the world unless he has attained this state of mind.

Almost no feature of Christian character is more striking or more decisive than indifference to the world's opinions. Since I have been in the ministry, I have been blessed with the acquaintance of some men who were particularly distinguished by this quality. I am thinking of one man especially. He seemed to have the least possible inclination to secure the applause of men or to avoid their censure. It seemed to be of no consequence to him to commend himself to men. For him, it was enough if he might please God.

Therefore, I was sure to find him in everlasting war against sin—all sin—however popular, however entrenched by custom, however sustained by wealth or public opinion. Yet he always opposed sin with a most remarkable spirit—a spirit of inflexible decision and yet of great mellowness and tenderness. While he was saying the most severe things in the most decided language, I often saw big tears rolling down his cheeks.

It is wonderful that most men never complained of his having a bad spirit. As much as they dreaded his rebuke and writhed under his strong and daring exposures of wickedness, they could never say that he did not have a good spirit. This spirit was a most beautiful and striking example of his having overcome the world.

Those who are not dead to the world, as this man was, have not escaped its bondage. The victorious Christian is in a state where he is no longer in bondage to man. He is bound only to serve God.

Chapter 5

Who Overcomes the World, and Why?

—◆—◆—

Now let us discuss our next question: who overcomes the world? Our text gives the answer: *"Everyone born of God overcomes the world"* (1 John 5:4 NIV). It is obvious that this is universal—*all* who are born of God overcome the world. All of these individuals overcome, and obviously it is implied that no one else overcomes. You may recognize those who are born of God by this characteristic—they overcome the world.

The next logical inquiry is, Why do believers overcome the world? By what principle do they overcome? I answer, This victory over the world is a natural result of the spiritual birth, just as bondage to the world is a natural result of the physical birth.

Entering the world by physical birth, and bondage to the world—these two things are connected by a law that is easy to explain and easy to understand. The law is as follows: physical birth reveals to the mind physical objects—and physical objects only. It brings the mind into contact with worldly things. It is, of course, natural for the mind to become deeply interested in these objects that are presented through the external senses. This is especially true because most of these objects have an intimate relationship with our senses and become the first and foremost sources of our happiness.

Therefore, our affections are gradually entwined around these objects, and we become avid lovers of this world before our eyes have looked upon it many months.

This law that I have explained is a universal fact. Now, there is another fact that is equally important and just as universal. It has to do with those powers of the mind that were created to take notice of our moral relationships and thereby counteract the bombardment of worldly objects. The truth is that these powers of the mind come into action very slowly. In fact, the amount of development that takes place with the moral-related powers in one year takes place with the object-related powers in probably one month. Hence, the moral-related powers are not very strong. Since the object-related powers are developed very early and are very strong, the soul is brought so entirely under the control of worldly objects that when the reason and the conscience speak up, their voice is given little attention. As a matter of fact, unless divine power intervenes, the soul's bondage to the world is never broken.

But the point that I particularly want to make clear is this: physical birth, with its laws of physical and mental development, becomes the occasion of bondage to this world.

I want to set side by side with this the birth into the kingdom of God by the Spirit. By this new birth, the soul is brought into intimate contact with spiritual things. The Spirit of God seems to usher the soul into the spiritual world. The result of the spiritual birth on our souls is exactly parallel to the result of the physical birth on our bodies. The great truths of the spiritual world are opened to our view through the illumination of the Spirit of God. We seem to see with new eyes and to have a new world of spiritual things all around us.

Regarding physical objects, men not only speculate about them, but also see them as real. Similarly, in the case of spiritual men, spiritual things become not merely matters of speculation, but matters of full and practical reality also. When God reveals Himself to the mind, spiritual things are seen in their real light and are seen to be reality.

Consequently, when spiritual things are thus revealed to the mind and are thus grasped, they will supremely interest that mind. Such is our mental makeup that when we thoroughly grasp the truth of God, it cannot fail to interest us. If these truths were clearly revealed to the wickedest man on earth so that he grasped them as realities, they could not fail to rouse his soul to most intense action. He might hate the light, he might stubbornly resist the claims of God upon his heart, but he could not fail to feel a strong interest in these truths that so take hold of the great and vital matters of human well-being.

Let me ask, Can there be a sinner on this wide earth who does not see that if God's presence were made as real to his mind as the presence of his fellowmen, it would supremely engross his soul, even though it might not subdue his heart? This revelation of God's presence and character might not convert him, but it would, at least for the time being, kill his attention to the world.

We often see this in the case of a person who is deeply convicted. Perhaps you have seen a person so fearfully convicted of sin that he cares nothing at all about his food or his clothes. "Oh," he cries out in the agony of his soul, "what will all these things matter to me, even if I get them all, if I must dwell in hell!"

Again, these piercing and all-absorbing convictions do not necessarily convert the soul. I have alluded to them here only to show the controlling power of the realization of divine truth.

When real conversion has taken place and the soul is born of God, then not only do realizations of truth awaken interest, as they might do in an unrenewed mind, but they also tend to excite a deep and ardent love for these truths. They draw out the heart. Spiritual truth now takes possession of the mind and draws the believer into its warm and life-giving embrace. Previously, error, falsehood, and death had drawn him under their power, but now the Spirit of God draws him into the very embrace of God. Now he is born of God and breathes the spirit of sonship. (See Romans 8:15.) Now, according to the Bible, God's *"seed remains in him"* (1 John 3:9). That very truth and those movings of the Spirit that gave him birth into the kingdom of God continue to have a powerful effect on his mind. Hence, he continues to be a Christian, and, as the Bible states, *"He cannot sin, because he has been born of God"* (v. 9). The seed of God is in him, and the fruit of it brings his soul into deep harmony with his own Father in heaven.

Again, the first birth acquaints us with earthly things; the second birth acquaints us with God. The first birth makes us acquainted with the finite, the second birth with the infinite. The first introduces us to things connected with our human nature, the second to those great things connected with our spiritual nature. These spiritual things are so lovely and so glorious that they overcome all the entanglements of the world.

Again, the first birth produces a worldly nature, and the second birth produces a heavenly nature. In the first birth, the mind is brought into a snare. In the second birth, it is delivered from that snare. Under the first birth, our citizenship is on earth. Under the second birth, *our citizenship is in heaven*" (Philippians 3:20).

Chapter 6

How Do We Overcome the World?

———◆◆◆———

How is this victory over the world achieved? The great agent is the Holy Spirit. Without Him, no good result is ever achieved in the Christian's heart or life. You will notice that the text says, *"This is the victory that has overcome the world, even our faith"* (1 John 5:4 NIV). But here the question might be raised, Does this mean that faith itself overcomes the world, or does this mean that we overcome the world through our faith? Undoubtedly, the latter is the precise meaning. By truly believing in God and having real impressions of His truth and character made upon our minds by the Holy Spirit, we gain victory over the world.

Faith involves three things: first, the perception of truth; second, an interest in it; third, the commitment of the mind to be interested in and controlled by the truths that faith perceives.

Perception of the truth must come first, for we cannot believe a truth that we do not know or perceive. Next, there must be an interest in the truth that will wake up the mind to focused and active attention. And third, there must be a voluntary commitment of the mind to be controlled by truth. The mind must wholly yield itself up to God to be governed entirely by His will. It must trust Him and Him alone as its present and eternal portion.

Faith receives Christ. The mind first perceives Christ's character and how He relates to us; it sees what He does for us. Then, when the soul deeply feels its need of such a Savior and such an inner work as He alone can do, it goes forth to receive and embrace Jesus as its own Savior. This action of the soul in receiving and embracing Christ is not sluggish; it is not done in a state of sleepy passivity. No, it involves the soul's most strenuous activity. This commitment of the soul must become a glorious, living, energizing principle. Not only must the mind perceive, but it must yield itself up with the most fervid intensity to be Christ's and to receive into the soul all the benefits of His salvation.

Again, faith receives Christ into the soul as King—to rule over the whole being; to receive the heart's supreme confidence and affection; to receive its obedience and adoration; in short, to rule over it and fulfill all the functions of supreme King over the whole moral being. We receive Christ into our very souls to live and to energize us there, to reign there forever on His own rightful throne.

Now, a great many people seem to stop short of this entire commitment of their entire souls to Christ. They stop short, perhaps, with merely perceiving the truth, satisfied and pleased that they have learned the theory of the Gospel. Perhaps some go one step further and stop with being interested—with having their feelings excited by the things of the Gospel. Thus, they go only to the second stage. Or perhaps they seem to receive faith but not Christ. They have some sort of belief in their minds but, after all, do not sincerely and with the entire heart welcome Christ Himself into the soul. All these various steps stop short of really taking hold of Christ. Not one of them results in obtaining victory over the world.

The true Bible doctrine of faith represents Christ as coming into the very soul. *"Behold, I stand at the door and knock. If anyone hears My voice and opens the door, I will come in to him and dine with him, and he with Me"* (Revelation 3:20). What could more powerfully and beautifully teach the doctrine that by faith Christ is introduced into the very soul of the believer to dwell there by His gracious presence?

Ever since my mind has been drawn to this subject, I have been astonished to see how long I have been dim-sighted in respect to this particular view of faith. For a long time I scarcely saw it. Now I see it beaming forth in lines of glory on almost every page of Scripture. The Bible seems to blaze with the glorious truth of *"Christ in* [the soul], *the hope of glory"* (Colossians 1:27), of God dwelling in our bodies as in a temple (1 Corinthians 3:16). I am amazed that a truth so rich and so blessed and so plainly revealed in the Bible was so dim to my sight. Christ received into the very soul by faith and thus brought into the nearest possible relationship to our hearts and lives; Christ Himself becoming the all-sustaining power within us by which we gain victory over the world; Christ living in and energizing our hearts—this is the great central truth in the plan of sanctification. Because believers value victory over the world and the living communion of the soul with its Maker, no Christian should fail to understand this truth.

Valuable Truths about Overcoming the World

If faith receives Christ into the soul, it is impossible for the soul not to overcome the world. Since the new birth actually brings the mind into this new state and brings Christ into the soul, then, of course, Christ will reign in the soul. The supreme affections will be yielded most delightfully to Him. The power of the world over the mind will be broken. Christ cannot dwell in any soul without absorbing the supreme interest of that soul. And this is, of course, equivalent to obtaining victory over the world.

He who does not habitually overcome the world is not born of God. In saying this, I do not mean that a true Christian may not sometimes be overcome by sin. But I do mean that overcoming the world is the general rule, and falling into sin is only the exception. This is the least that can be meant by our text and by similar statements that are found throughout the Bible. Take, for instance, 1 John 3:9: *"Whoever has been born of God does not sin...and he cannot sin, because he has been born of God."* Nothing less can be meant than this, that he cannot sin constantly, cannot make sinning his business, and can sin, if at all, only occasionally and aside from the general current of his life. In the same way, we would say of a man who is generally truthful that he is not a liar.

I will not contend for more than this regarding either our text or 1 John 3:9, but for this much I must contend. The newly born souls spoken of in these verses do in general overcome the world. The general fact regarding them is that they do not sin and are not in bondage to Satan. At the very least, their general character must coincide with the Scripture's assertions about them.

What good is a religion that does not overcome the world? What is the benefit of being born into such a religion if it leaves the world still ruling over our hearts? What help is a new birth that, after all, fails to bring us into a likeness to God, fails to bring us into harmony with His family and His kingdom, fails to break our bondage to the world and to Satan? What more can there be to such a religion than a mere name? How can any man suppose that such a religion prepares his heart for heaven when it leaves him earthly-minded, fleshly, and selfish?

The Meaning of True Christianity

Thus we see why infidels have proclaimed the Gospel of Christ to be a failure. They maintain that it claims to bring men out of the world but fails to do so, and hence is evidently a failure. Now, you must observe that the Bible does indeed affirm, as infidels say, that those who are truly born of God do overcome the world. This we cannot deny, and should not wish to deny. Now, if the infidel can show that the new birth fails to produce this result, he has proven his point, and we must yield ours. This is perfectly plain, and there can be no escape for us.

But the infidel's premises are faulty. He assumes that the current Christianity of the age is a specimen of real religion, and he builds his estimate on this. He thinks that he proves, and perhaps he truly does prove, that the current Christianity does not overcome the world.

We must object to his assuming that this current type of Christianity is real religion, for this religion of nominal Christians does not fit the descriptions of true piety in God's Word. Moreover, if this current type of religion were all that the Gospel and the Divine Spirit could do for lost man, we might as well yield this point to the infidel; for such a religion could not give us much evidence of having come from God and would be of very little value to man—so little that it would scarcely be worth contending for. Truly, if we must take the professedly Christian world as Bible Christians, who would not be ashamed and perplexed in attempting to confront the infidel? We know all too well that the great majority of professing Christians do not overcome the world, and we would be defeated quickly if we were to maintain that they do. Those professing Christians themselves know that they do not overcome the world. They could not testify that the power of the Gospel is displayed in their own cases.

In view of facts like these, I have often been astonished to see ministers attempting to persuade their people that they are really converted, trying to soothe their fears and sustain their tottering hopes. Futile effort! Those same ministers, it would seem, must know that they themselves do not overcome the world, and they must know equally well that their people do not. How fatal to the soul, then, must be such efforts to heal *"the hurt of* [God's professed] *people slightly, saying, 'Peace, peace!' when there is no peace"* (Jeremiah 6:14).

Let us get to the bottom of this matter, pressing the question, Do the great majority of professing Christians really overcome the world? It is a fact beyond question that, with them, the things of this world are the realities and the things of God are mere theories. Who does not know that this is the real state of great multitudes in the nominal church?

Let this searching question penetrate your heart: What are the things that set your soul on fire, that stir up your most fervent emotions? Are these the things of earth or the things of heaven? The things of time or the things of eternity? The things of self or the things of God?

What happens when you go into your prayer closet? Do you go there to seek and find God? Do you in fact find there a present God, and do you hold communion there as friend with friend? What happens?

Now, you certainly should know that if your state is such that spiritual things are mere theories and speculations, you are altogether worldly and nothing more. It would be outright foolishness and falsehood to call you spiritually-minded, and for you to think of yourself as spiritual would be the most fatal and foolish self-deception. You give none of the appropriate proofs of being born of God. Your state is not that of one who is personally acquainted with God and who loves Him personally with supreme affection.

Until we can put away from the minds of men the common error that the current Christianity of the church is true Christianity, we can make very little progress in converting the world. In the first place, unless we eradicate this error, we cannot save the church itself from bondage to the world in this life or from the direst doom of the hypocrite in the next. We cannot unite and arm the church in vigorous attack on Satan's kingdom, so that the world may be converted to God. We cannot even convince intelligent men of the world that our religion is from God and brings to fallen men a remedy for their depravity. For if the common Christianity of the age is the best that can be, and this does not give men the victory over the world, what good is it? And if it really is of little worth or none, how can we hope to make thinking men prize it as something of great value?

There are very few infidels who are as much in the dark on these points as they claim to be. Most of them are acquainted with some humble Christians whose lives commend Christianity and condemn the infidel's ungodliness. These infidels know the truth, that there is a reality in the religion of the Bible, and they blind their own eyes selfishly and most foolishly when they try to believe that the religion of the Bible is a failure and that the Bible is therefore a fabrication. Deep in their hearts lies the conviction that here and there are real Christians who overcome the world and live by a faith unknown to themselves. In how many cases does God set some burning examples of Christian life before those wicked, skeptical men to rebuke them for their sin and their skepticism—perhaps their own wives or their children, their neighbors or their coworkers? By such means the truth is lodged in their minds, and God has a witness for Himself in their consciences.

I will tell a true story that occurred in the South and was shared with me by a minister of the Gospel who was acquainted with the circumstances of the case. There resided in that region a very worldly and a most ungodly man who had many slaves and was given over to horse racing. Heedless of all religion and openly skeptical, he gave full sway to every evil tendency. But wicked men must one day see trouble, and this man became very sick and was brought to the very gates of the grave. His weeping wife and friends gathered around his bed and began to think of having some Christian called in to pray for the dying man's soul.

"Husband," said the anxious wife, "shouldn't I send for our minister to pray with you before you die?" "No," said he. "I've known him a long time, and I have no confidence in him. I have seen him too many times at horse races. There he was my friend and I was his, but I don't want to see him now."

"But who will we get, then?" continued the wife. "Send for my slave Tom," he replied. "He is one of my stablemen. I have often overheard him praying, and I know he can pray. Besides, I have watched his life, and I have never seen anything in him inconsistent with Christian character. Call him in. I would be glad to hear him pray."

Tom came in slowly and respectfully, took off his hat at the door, and looked at his sick and dying master. "Tom," said the dying skeptic, "can you pray for your dying master and forgive him?" "Oh yes, Master, with all my heart." Tom dropped to his knees and poured out a prayer for his soul.

Now, the moral of this story is obvious. Place the skeptic on his deathbed, let that solemn hour arrive and the inner convictions of his heart be revealed, and he knows of at least one man who is a Christian. He knows one man whose prayers he values more than all the friendships of his former associates. He knows now that there is such a thing as Christianity. Yet do not suppose that he has just this moment learned a lesson he never knew before. No, he knew just as much before. An honest hour has simply brought the inner convictions of his soul to light. Infidels generally know more than they are honest enough to admit.

The Great Error of Many in the Church

The great error of those who profess religion but are not born of God is this: they are trying to be Christians without being born of God. They need to have done to them what is said of Adam: *"The LORD God…breathed into* [him] *the breath of life; and man became a living soul"* (Genesis 2:7 KJV). Their religion has in it none of the breath of God. It is a cold, lifeless theory. There is none of the living vitality of God in it. Even though they may flatter themselves that their creed is sound, do they love the truth that they profess to believe? They think, perhaps, that they have zeal and that their zeal is right and that their hearts are right, but are their souls on fire for God and His cause?

Where are they, and what are they doing? Are they spinning out some favorite theory, or are they defending it at the point of the sword? Ah, do they care about souls? Do their hearts tremble for the interests of Zion? Do their very nerves quiver under the mighty power of God's truth? Does their love for God and for souls set their orthodoxy and their creeds on fire so that every truth burns in their souls and glows forth from their very faces?

If so, you will not see them absent from the prayer meetings. On the contrary, you will see that divine things take hold of their souls with overwhelming interest and power. You will see that they are truly Christians, burning and shining lights in the world. Dear reader, it cannot be too strongly impressed on every mind that the decisive characteristic of true religion is energy, not apathy. Its vital essence is life, not death.

PART THREE

Christ, Our Sanctification

Sanctify is a term frequently used in the Bible. Simply put, sanctification is a state of consecration to God. To sanctify is to set apart for holy use—to consecrate a thing or person to the service of God.

Entire sanctification implies entire conformity of heart and life to all the known will of God. Love is the sum of all that is implied in entire sanctification. Our love for God must be supreme. If anything is loved more than God, that is our god.

A state of entire sanctification can never be attained by the formation of holy habits, nor by any effort to have the right kind of feelings, nor by attempting to copy the experience of others. This state is to be attained by faith alone. It is based alone on the grace of God in Jesus Christ.

While individuals are taken up with contemplating themselves, their own characters, their own dangers, and their own troubles, they cannot be sanctified. It is a consideration of the infinite excellence of Christ's character, and this alone, that can inspire faith or love. God, and not yourself, must be the object of your thoughts.

Chapter 7

Christic, Our King

❖ ◆ ❖

For the LORD Most High is awesome; He is a great
King over all the earth.
—Psalm 47:2

Before we look in depth at the subject of sanctification, we need to look at the temptations that overcome us.

When a person is first converted, the heart or will consecrates itself and the whole being to God. This is a commitment of the whole being to the promotion of the highest good of being. All sin, on the other hand, is selfishness. All sin lies in the will seeking the indulgence or gratification of self. It lies in the will yielding obedience to the sinful inclinations instead of obeying God as His law is revealed in the reason.

Now, what needs to be done to break the power of temptation and let the soul go free? In order to answer this question, we will consider the sensibility—the part of the mind that feels, desires, suffers, enjoys. The fact is that the department of our sensibility that is related to temporal and sensory things has developed enormously and is tremblingly alive to all that corresponds to it. Meanwhile, because of the blindness of the mind to spiritual things, it is scarcely developed at all in its relationship to them. Spiritual things are seldom thought of by the carnal mind (see Romans 7:14), and when they are, they are only thought of; they are not clearly seen and, of course, are not felt.

Thoughts of God, of Christ, of sin, of holiness, of heaven, and of hell excite little or no emotion in the carnal mind. The carnal mind is alive and awake to earthly and tangible objects but is dead to spiritual realities. This is why the spiritual world needs to be revealed to the soul. The soul needs to see and clearly understand its own spiritual condition, necessities, and relationships. It needs to become acquainted with God and Christ, to have spiritual and eternal realities made plain, present, and all-absorbing realities. The soul needs revelations of the eternal world—of the nature and guilt of sin, and of Christ, the Remedy of the soul—that will kill its lusts and awaken it to spiritual realities. This will greatly diminish the frequency and power of the temptations to gratify self, and will break up the voluntary slavery of the will.

The developments of the sensibility need to be thoroughly corrected. This can be done only by the Holy Spirit's revelation to the inward man of those great, solemn, and overpowering realities of the "spirit land"—realities that lie concealed from the eye of flesh.

We often see those around us whose sensibility is so developed in one or more directions that they are led captive by appetite and passion in those directions in spite of reason and of God. The alcoholic is an example of this. People who are gluttonous, immoral, or greedy are also examples of this.

On the other hand, we sometimes see, by some striking providence, a counter-development of the sensibility that slays those particular tendencies. The whole direction of a man's life seems to be changed, at least outwardly. From being a perfect slave to his appetite for alcohol, he cannot, without the utmost loathing and disgust, so much as hear the name of his once-loved beverage mentioned. From being a very greedy man, he becomes deeply disgusted with wealth and spurns and despises it. Now, this has been brought about by a counter-development of the sensibility. It is an outward change only. In this particular case, religion had nothing to do with it.

However, because sin consists of the will being influenced by the sensibility, one great thing that needs to be done to strengthen and settle the will in the attitude of entire consecration to God is this: a spiritual counter-development of the sensibility must be brought about, so that it will not draw the will away from God. The sensibility needs to be crucified to the world, to things of time and sense, by a deep, clear, and powerful revelation of self to self and of Christ to the soul. This will awaken and develop all of the soul's sensitivity to Christ and to spiritual and divine realities. This can be done easily through and by the Holy Spirit, who takes the things of Christ and shows them to us (John 16:14).

The Holy Spirit so reveals Christ that the soul receives Him to the throne of the heart, to reign throughout the whole being. When the will, the intellect, and the sensibility are yielded to Christ, He develops the intelligence and the sensibility by clear revelations of Himself, in all His offices and roles, to the soul. He strengthens the will and mellows and chastens the sensibility by these divine revelations to the intelligence.

It is plain that men are naturally able to be entirely sanctified in the sense of rendering entire and continual obedience to God, for men would not be obligated to do something they cannot do. But what is implied in the ability to be as holy as God requires us to be? Clearly, it is implied that we must have sufficient knowledge or light to plainly reveal to us the means of overcoming every difficulty or temptation that lies in our way. This knowledge is offered to us on the condition that we receive the Holy Spirit, who offers Himself as an indwelling light and guide and is received by simple faith.

The light and grace that we need and that it is the office of the Holy Spirit to supply concerns mainly the following things:

1. The knowledge of ourselves and of our past sins—their nature, guilt, and desert of dire damnation

2. The knowledge of our spiritual helplessness or weakness as a result of the following: the physical depravity of our natures, the strength of selfish habit, and the power of temptation from the world, the flesh, and the devil

3. The knowledge of the character of God, the nature of His government, the purity of His law, and the necessity and fact of atonement for sin

4. The knowledge of our need of Christ in all His offices and roles

5. The revelation of Christ to our souls in all these roles, and in the great power that will produce in us a faith that takes hold of Him, without which Christ is not and cannot be our salvation

We need to know Christ in His many roles, and I will discuss these roles throughout the remainder of this book.

King

We need to see and receive Christ as our King. In this position, His role is to set up His government and to write His law in our hearts (Jeremiah 31:33); to establish His kingdom within us; to sway His scepter over our whole being. He must be spiritually revealed and received as King.

Mediator

We also need to know Christ as our Mediator. As such, His role is to stand between the offended justice of God and our guilty souls, to bring about a reconciliation between our souls and God. He must be known and received as Mediator.

Advocate

Our Advocate, our best Friend to plead our cause with the Father, our righteous and all-prevailing Advocate to secure the triumph of our cause in the courtroom of God—in this relationship He must be seen and embraced.

Redeemer

We need to have Christ revealed to us as our Redeemer. In this position, His role is to redeem us from the curse of the law (Galatians 3:13) and from the power and dominion of sin, to pay the price demanded by public justice for our release, and to overcome and break up forever our spiritual bondage. In this role, also, we must know and appreciate Him by faith.

Our Justification

We also need to view Christ as our Justification. His role here is to procure our pardon and acceptance with God. To know Him and embrace Him in this relationship is indispensable to peace of mind and to release from the condemnation of the law.

Judge

Christ is our Judge, who pronounces upon us a sentence of acceptance and awards us the victor's crown. (See 2 Timothy 4:8.)

Repairer of the Breach

We also need Christ to be revealed to the soul as *"the Repairer of the Breach"* (Isaiah 58:12), or as the One who makes good to the government of God our default. In other words, Christ is the One who, by His obedience unto death, rendered to the public justice of God a full governmental equivalent of the infliction of the penalty of the law upon us.

The Propitiation

We need to see and receive Christ as *"the propitiation for our sins"* (1 John 2:2). As such, His role was to give Himself as an offering for our sins. Seeing Christ as atoning for our sins seems to be indispensable to a healthy hope of eternal life. It certainly is not healthy for the soul to contemplate the mercy of God without realizing that Christ had to die so that we could receive that mercy. Unless a person sees that Christ offered Himself to atone for our sins, his soul is not sufficiently impressed with a sense of the justice and holiness of God, or with the guilt and deserved punishment of sin. A person is not awed and humbled in the deepest dust if he regards God as extending pardon without regarding the sternness of His justice. As a condition of granting forgiveness for sin, God requires that sin be recognized in the universe as worthy of His wrath and curse.

It is remarkable and well worthy of consideration that those who deny the Atonement see sin as something small and insignificant. They seem to regard God's benevolence or love as good nature rather than, as it is, *"a consuming fire"* (Hebrews 12:29) to all the workers of iniquity. Nothing does or can produce that awe of God, that fear and holy dread of sin, that self-abasing, God-exalting spirit, that a thorough understanding of the atonement of Christ will. Like nothing else, this can produce that spirit of self-renunciation, of cleaving to Christ, of taking refuge in His blood. In this role, Christ must be revealed to us, perceived by us, and embraced by us, as the condition of our entire sanctification.

The Guarantee of a Better Covenant

We also need to know Christ as the Guarantee of a covenant that is better than the first covenant. That is, He is the Guarantee of a gracious covenant founded on better promises (Hebrews 8:6). Christ is the underwriter or endorser of our obligation. He is the One who undertakes for us; He pledges Himself as our security to fulfill for us and in us all the conditions of our salvation. To see and receive Christ by faith in this role is no doubt a condition of our entire sanctification.

Our Substitute

We need to see and receive Christ as dying for our sins. It is the work of the Holy Spirit to reveal Christ's death in its relationship to our individual sins and to our sins as individuals. Our souls need to see Christ as crucified *for us*. It is one thing for the soul to regard the death of Christ merely as the death of a martyr; and it is an infinitely different thing, as everyone knows who has had the experience, to recognize His death as a real, vicarious sacrifice for our sins, as being truly a substitute for our death. The soul needs to see Christ as suffering on the cross for it as its Substitute so that it can say, "That sacrifice is for me; that suffering and that death are for my sins. The Blessed Lamb is slain for my sins." If fully seeing and receiving Christ cannot kill sin in us, what can?

A Risen and Justifying Savior

We also need to know Christ as risen for our justification (Romans 4:25 KJV). He arose and lives to obtain our certain acquittal, our complete pardon and acceptance with God. We need to know that He lives and is our Justification in order to break the bondage of wrong motives, to slay all selfish fear, and to break and destroy the power of temptation from these sources. The soul is often tempted to despondency and unbelief, to despair of its own acceptance with God. It would surely fall into the bondage of fear were it not for faith in Christ as a risen, living, justifying Savior.

Our Sorrow-Bearer

We also need to have Christ revealed to us as bearing our griefs and carrying our sorrows (Isaiah 53:4). The clear understanding of Christ as being made sorrowful for us, and as bending under sorrows and griefs that justly belonged to us, tends at once to render sin unspeakably horrid and Christ infinitely precious to our souls. The idea of Christ as our substitute Sorrow-Bearer needs to be thoroughly developed in our minds. And this role of Christ needs to be so clearly revealed to us that it becomes an ever present reality to us. We need to have Christ so revealed to us that He completely captivates and engrosses our affections.

Our Healer

We also need to see Christ as the One by whose stripes we are healed (Isaiah 53:5). We need to know Him as relieving our pains and sufferings by His own suffering, as preventing our death by His own death, as sorrowing so that we might eternally rejoice, as grieving so that we might be unspeakably and eternally glad, as dying in unspeakable agony so that we might die in deep peace and unspeakable triumph.

Sin for Us

Christ was made sin for us (2 Corinthians 5:21). We need to see Him as being treated as a sinner, even as the chief of sinners, for us. Scripture teaches that, on our account, Christ was treated as if He were a sinner. He was made sin for us; He consented to take our place in such a sense as to endure the Cross, and the curse of the law, for us. When the soul understands this, it is ready to die with grief and love. Oh, how infinitely it loathes self under such a realization as this! In this role of sin for us, Christ must not only be seen but also received by faith.

The One Who Makes Us Righteous

We also need to grasp the fact that Christ was made sin for us so that *"we might become the righteousness of God in Him"* (2 Corinthians 5:21). Christ was treated as a sinner so that we might be treated as righteous; so that we might also be made personally righteous by faith in Him; so that *"we might become the righteousness of God in Him"*; so that we might inherit and be made partakers of God's righteousness as that righteousness exists and is revealed in Christ; so that we might in and by Him be made righteous as God is righteous. The soul needs to see that His being made sin for us was in order that *"we might become the righteousness of God in Him."* By faith, the soul needs to embrace and lay hold of the righteousness of God that is brought home to believers in Christ through the Atonement and the indwelling Spirit.

The Administrator of the World's Government

We also need Him to be revealed to the soul as the One upon whose shoulders is the government of the world (Isaiah 9:6), who administers the moral and providential government of this world for the protection, discipline, and benefit of believers. This revelation has a most sin-subduing tendency. That all events are directly or indirectly controlled by Him who has so loved us that He has died for us; that all things are absolutely designed for and will surely result in our good— these and similar considerations, when revealed to the soul and made living realities by the Holy Spirit, tend to kill selfishness and strengthen the love of God in the soul.

Head over All

We also need Christ to be revealed to the inward being as *"head over all things to the church"* (Ephesians 1:22). But it is one thing to have thoughts and ideas and opinions concerning Christ and an entirely different thing to know Christ as He is revealed by the Holy Spirit. All the roles of Christ imply corresponding needs in us. The Holy Spirit reveals to us our need and then reveals Christ as exactly suited to meet that need. The Holy Spirit then urges us to accept Him in that role until we have received Him by faith.

Many who profess to be Christians know Christ only *"according to the flesh"* (2 Corinthians 5:16). They think sanctification is brought about by forming holy habits instead of by, first, the revelation of Christ to the soul in all His fullness and roles, and second, the soul's renunciation of self and acceptance of Christ in these roles. The utter darkness of the human mind in regard to its own spiritual state and needs, and in regard to the roles and fullness of Christ, is truly astounding. His roles as mentioned in the Bible are overlooked almost entirely until we discover our needs. When these are made known and the soul begins in earnest to seek a remedy, it need not seek in vain.

The Possessor of All Power

Christ as having all power or authority in heaven and earth (Matthew 28:18) needs also to be revealed to the soul and received by it through faith, to dwell in and rule over it. It is essential that the corresponding need be known to the mind before the soul can see and receive Christ by faith in this or any other role. The soul needs to see and feel its weakness, its need of being protected, defended, watched over, and controlled. It also needs to see the power of its spiritual enemies, its troubles, its dangers, and its certain ruin unless the almighty One intervenes on its behalf. The soul needs to truly and deeply know itself in this way. Then, to inspire the soul with confidence, it needs a revelation of Christ as God, as the almighty God, as the One who possesses absolute and infinite power, and as the One who is presented to the soul to be accepted as its strength and as all the power it needs.

Oh, how infinitely blind a person is to the fullness and glory of Christ if he does not know himself and know Christ as both are revealed by the Holy Spirit! When self, in all its loathsomeness and helplessness, is fully revealed until all hope of finding any help in self is gone—and when Christ, the All in All, is revealed to the soul as its all-sufficient portion and salvation— then, and not until then, does the soul know its salvation. This knowledge is the indispensable condition of appropriating faith—the act of receiving Christ and committing all to Him that brings Him home to dwell in the heart by faith and to preside over all its states and actions. But it is one thing to theorize and speculate about Christ, and an infinitely different thing to *know* Him as He is revealed by the Holy Spirit.

When Christ is fully revealed to the soul by the Comforter, it will never again doubt the attainability and reality of entire sanctification in this life.

Chapter 8

Christize, the Prince of Peace

◆━◆━◆

And His name will be called Wonderful, Counselor,
Mighty God, Everlasting Father, Prince of Peace.
—Isaiah 9:6

Another necessity of the soul is to know Christ
spiritually as the Prince of Peace. Christ said,
"Peace I leave with you, My peace I give to you" (John
14:27). What is this peace? And who is Christ
in the role of the Prince of Peace? What does
it mean to possess the peace of Christ—to have
the peace of God rule in our hearts (Colossians
3:15)? Unless Christ is revealed to the soul by
the Holy Spirit, it has no spiritual comprehension
of what this means. Nor can it lay hold of and
receive Christ as its peace, as the Prince of Peace.
Whoever knows and has embraced Christ as his

peace and as the Prince of Peace knows what it is to have the peace of God rule in his heart. But no one else understands the true spiritual import of this language, nor can it be explained to him in such a way that he will understand it unless it is explained by the Holy Spirit.

The Captain of Salvation

The soul also needs to know Christ as the Captain of Salvation (Hebrews 2:10), as the skillful conductor and guide of the soul in all its conflicts with its spiritual enemies. Jesus Christ is ever at hand to lead the soul on to victory and make it more than a conqueror in all its conflicts with the world, the flesh, and the devil. In order for a person to have a living and effective faith, it is indispensable for the soul to clearly understand by the Holy Spirit this role of Captain of Salvation and Captain of the Lord's Host (Joshua 5:15 KJV). Without confidence in the Leader and Captain, how could the soul put itself under His guidance and protection in the hour of conflict? It could not.

The fact is that when the soul is ignorant of Christ as its Captain or Leader, it will surely fall in battle. If the church as a body only knew Christ as the Captain of the Lord's Host, if He were only truly and spiritually known to them in that role, no more confusion would be seen in the ranks of God's elect. All would be order and strength and conquest. They would soon go up and take possession of the whole territory that has been promised to Christ. The heathen would soon be given to Him for an inheritance, and the uttermost parts of the world for a possession (Psalm 2:8).

Our Passover

Another important role in which the soul needs to know Christ is that of our Passover (1 Corinthians 5:7). The soul needs to understand that the only reason that it has not been or will not be slain for sin is that Christ, our Passover Lamb, has sprinkled the lintel and doorposts of our souls with His own blood, and that therefore the destroying angel passes us by. (See Exodus 12:21–23.)

There is a deep and sin-subduing, or rather temptation-subduing, spirituality in this role of Christ to the soul when revealed by the Holy Spirit. We must see our sins as slaying the Lamb, and we must apply His blood to our souls by faith—His blood as our only hope. We need to know the security there is in being sprinkled with His blood, and the certain and speedy destruction of all who have not taken refuge under it. We also need to know that it will not do for a moment to venture out into the streets without its protection, lest we be slain there.

Our Wisdom

To know Christ as our Wisdom in the true spiritual sense is indispensable to our entire—in the sense of continued—sanctification. He is our Wisdom in that He is the whole of our religion. That is, when separated from Him, we have no spiritual life whatsoever. He is at the bottom of, or the inducing cause of, all our obedience.

Our Sanctification

Very closely allied to this is Christ's relationship to the soul as its Sanctification. I have been amazed at the ignorance of the church and the ministry concerning Christ as our Sanctification. He is not our Sanctifier in the sense that He does something to the soul that enables it to stand and persevere in holiness in its own strength. He does not change the structure of the soul. Rather, He watches over it and works in it both to will and to do continually (Philippians 2:13). In this way, He becomes its Sanctification. His influence is not exerted once and for all, but constantly.

When Christ is understood and embraced as the soul's Sanctification, He rules in and reigns over the soul in so high a sense that He, as it were, develops His own holiness in us. He, as it were, swallows us up. He so enfolds (if I may express it this way) our wills and our souls in His that we are willingly led captive by Him. We will and do as He wills within us. He beautifully draws the will into a universal bending to His will. He so establishes His throne in us and His authority over us that He subdues us to Himself. However, He becomes our Sanctification only insofar as we are revealed to ourselves and He is revealed to us, and only insofar as we receive Him and put Him on (Galatians 3:27).

What! Has it come to this, that the church doubts and rejects the doctrine of entire sanctification in this life? Then it must be that they have lost sight of Christ as their Sanctification. Is not Christ perfect in all His roles? Is there not a completeness and fullness in Him? When He is embraced by us, are we not complete in Him? The reason for all this doubting about and opposition to the doctrine of entire sanctification is that Christ is not recognized and embraced as our Sanctification. The Holy Spirit sanctifies only by revealing Christ to us as our Sanctification. The Holy Spirit does not speak of Himself, but He takes of the things of Christ and shows them to us (John 16:13–14).

Our Redemption

Another of Christ's spiritual roles is that of the Redemption of the soul. Not only is He the Redeemer, but He is a present redemption. To see and receive Christ in this role, the soul needs to see itself as *"sold as a slave to sin"* (Romans 7:14

NIV), as being the voluntary but real slave of lust and appetite—except as Christ continually delivers it from sin's power by strengthening its will in resisting and overcoming the flesh.

Our Prophet

Christ our Prophet is another important spiritual relationship in which we need to comprehend Christ by the Holy Spirit as a condition of entire sanctification. Christ must be received as the great Teacher of our souls so that every word of His will be received as God speaking to us. This will render the Bible precious and all the words of life effective to the sanctification of our souls.

Our High Priest

We also need to know Christ as our High Priest (Hebrews 4:14). We need to know that He ever lives and ever sustains this relationship to us, offering up, as it were, by a continual offering, His own blood and Himself as a propitiation for our sins. He has entered within the veil and ever lives to make intercession for us (Hebrews 7:25). Much precious instruction is to be gathered from this role of Christ. We need, desperately need, to know Christ in this role in order to have a right dependence on Him.

When we sin, it is because of our ignorance of Christ. That is, whenever temptation overcomes us, it is because we do not know and avail ourselves of that role of Christ that would meet our necessities at the time. One thing that needs to be done is to correct the development of our appetites and passions, which are enormously developed in their relationship to earthly things. In relationship to things of time and sense, our inclinations are greatly developed and are alive. However, in relationship to spiritual truths and eternal realities, we are naturally as dead as stones.

When a person is first converted, if he knows enough about himself and about Christ to thoroughly correct and develop the action of his appetites and to strengthen his will in a state of entire consecration, he should not fall. To the degree that the law-work preceding conversion has been thorough and the revelation of Christ at or immediately subsequent to conversion has been full and clear, to that same degree do we witness stability in converts. In most instances, if not in all, however, the convert is too ignorant of himself, and, of course, knows too little about Christ to be established in permanent obedience. He needs renewed conviction of sin revealed to him, and he needs Christ revealed to him. Christ must be formed in him as *"the hope of glory"* (Colossians 1:27) before he will be *"steadfast, immovable, always abounding in the work of the Lord"* (1 Corinthians 15:58).

It must not be inferred that knowing Christ in all these roles is a condition of our coming into a state of entire consecration to God, or of present sanctification. The thing I insist on is that the soul will abide in this state in the hour of temptation only insofar as it takes itself to Christ, and only insofar as it sees and receives Him by faith in those roles that meet its present, pressing needs. The temptation is the occasion of revealing the need, and the Holy Spirit is always ready to reveal Christ in the particular role suited to the newly developed need. The realization and acceptance of Him in this role, under these circumstances of trial, is absolutely essential to our remaining in the state of entire consecration.

The Bread of Life

We also need to know ourselves as starving souls and Christ as the Bread of Life (John 6:35), as *"the bread which came down from heaven"* (v. 41). We need to know spiritually and personally what it is to eat of His flesh and to drink of His blood (v. 53), to receive Him as the Bread of Life, to receive Him for the nourishment of our souls as truly as we receive and digest bread for the nourishment of our bodies. I know this sounds like mysticism to the carnal person who professes Christianity. But to the truly spiritually-minded, *"this is the bread which comes down from heaven, that one may eat of it and not die"* (v. 50).

To hear Christ talk of eating His flesh and of drinking His blood was a great stumbling block to the carnal Jews, as it is now to carnal professing Christians. Nevertheless, this is a glorious truth, that Christ is the constant sustenance of the spiritual life as truly and as literally as food is the sustenance of the body. But the soul will never eat this Bread until it has ceased to attempt to fill itself with the husks of its own doings, or with any provision this world can furnish. Do you know, Christian, what it is to eat of this Bread? If so, you will never die.

The Fountain of the Water of Life

Christ also needs to be revealed to the soul as the Fountain of the Water of Life. He said, *"If anyone thirsts, let him come to Me and drink"* (John 7:37), and, *"I am the Alpha and the Omega, the Beginning and the End. I will give of the fountain of the water of life freely to him who thirsts"* (Revelation 21:6).

The soul needs to have revelations that will produce a thirst for God—a thirst that cannot be quenched except by a plentiful drink at the Fountain of the Water of Life. In order for the soul to be established in perfect love, it is indispensable that its hungering after the Bread and its thirsting for the Water of Life be awakened. The soul must pant and struggle after God and cry out for the living God. The believer must be able to truthfully say, *"As the deer pants for the water brooks, so pants my soul for You, O God"* (Psalm 42:1). *"My heart and my flesh cry out for the living God"* (Psalm 84:2). *"My soul breaks with longing for* [You] *at all times"* (Psalm 119:20).

When this state of mind is induced by the Holy Spirit so that the longing of the soul after perpetual holiness is irrepressible, the soul is prepared for a revelation of Christ in all those offices and roles that are necessary to secure its establishment in love. It is then especially prepared to see, appreciate, and receive Christ as the Bread and Water of Life. The soul is ready to understand what it is to eat the flesh and drink the blood of the Son of God. (See John 6:53.) It is then in a state to understand what Christ meant when He said, *"Blessed are those who hunger and thirst for righteousness, for they shall be filled"* (Matthew 5:6); He meant that they understand not only what it is to hunger and thirst, but also what it is to be filled—to have the hunger and thirst allayed and the largest desire fully satisfied. The soul then realizes, in its own experience, the truthfulness of the apostle Paul's saying that Christ *"is able to do exceedingly abundantly above all that we ask or think"* (Ephesians 3:20).

Many stop short of anything even close to intense hunger and thirst. Others hunger and thirst but do not understand the perfect fullness and ability of Christ to meet and satisfy the longing of their souls. They, therefore, do not plead and look for the soul-satisfying revelation of Christ. They expect no such divine fullness and satisfaction of soul. They are ignorant of the fullness and perfection of the provisions of the *"glorious gospel of the blessed God"* (1 Timothy 1:11). Consequently, the fact that they hunger and thirst after righteousness does not encourage them to hope that they will be filled. Instead, they remain unfed, unfilled, unsatisfied. After a season, through unbelief, they fall into indifference and remain in bondage to lust.

The True God and the Eternal Life

The soul also needs to know Christ as *"the true God and eternal life"* (1 John 5:20). However, *"no one can say that Jesus is Lord except by the Holy Spirit"* (1 Corinthians 12:3). Christ's divinity never is and never can be held other than as a mere opinion, tenet, speculation, or article of a creed, until He is revealed to the inner man by the Holy Spirit. But nothing short of the soul's understanding of Christ as the supreme and living God can inspire the confidence in Him that is essential to the soul's established sanctification.

Until the soul spiritually knows Christ as the true God, it can have no comprehension of what is intended by His being the Eternal Life. When

He is spiritually revealed as the true and living God, the way is prepared for the spiritual understanding of Him as the Eternal Life.

All of the following verses were spoken either by Christ or of Christ: *"As the Father has life in Himself, so He has granted the Son to have life in Himself"* (John 5:26). *"In Him was life, and the life was the light of men"* (John 1:4). *"I give them eternal life"* (John 10:28). *"I am the way, the truth, and the life"* (John 14:6). *"I am the resurrection and the life"* (John 11:25). The soul needs to spiritually understand these and similar passages; the soul needs to have a spiritual and personal revelation of them within.

The Bible can be made of spiritual use to professing Christians only on a certain condition. Unfortunately, it seems to me that most professing Christians have no right idea of what this condition is. They do not seem to understand that the words of the Bible themselves are only a history of things formerly revealed to men; the Bible's words are, in fact, a revelation to no one unless they are personally revealed, or revealed to us in particular by the Holy Spirit. So it is with every spiritual truth. Without an inward revelation of it to the soul, it is only an *"aroma of death leading to death"* (2 Corinthians 2:16).

It is in vain for a person to hold to the divinity of Christ as a speculation, doctrine, theory, or opinion, without the revelation of His divine nature and character to the soul by the Holy Spirit. But let the soul know Him and walk with Him as the true God, and then it will no longer question whether, as our Sanctification, He is all-sufficient and complete.

Yet, let no one object that, if this is true, men are under no obligation to believe in Christ and to obey the Gospel unless or until they are enlightened by the Holy Spirit. If such an objection were made, I would answer two things.

First, men are under an obligation to believe every truth insofar as they can understand it, but no further. As far as they can understand the spiritual truths of the Gospel without the Holy Spirit, so far, without His aid, they are bound to believe them. But Christ Himself has taught us that no one can come to Him unless the Father draws him (John 6:44). This drawing is teaching. This is evident from what Christ proceeded to say,

> It is written in the prophets, "And they shall all be taught by God." Therefore everyone who has heard and learned from the Father comes to Me.   (John 6:45)

However, this "learn[ing] from the Father" is different from the mere oral or written instructions of Christ and the apostles. This is evident, for Christ assured those to whom He preached, with all the plainness with which He was able, that they still could not come to Him unless they were drawn—that is, taught—by the Father. As the Father teaches by the Holy Spirit, Christ's plain teaching in John 6:44–45 is that no one can come to Him unless he is specially enlightened by the Holy Spirit.

Paul unequivocally taught the same thing. *"No one,"* he said, *"can say that Jesus is Lord except by the Holy Spirit"* (1 Corinthians 12:3). Notwithstanding all the teaching of the apostles, no one by merely listening to their instruction could understand the true divinity of Christ in such a way that he could honestly and with spiritual understanding say that Jesus is Lord. But what spiritual or true Christian does not know the radical difference between being taught by man and being taught by God—between the opinions that we form from reading, hearing, and studying, and the clear understanding of truths that are communicated by the direct and inward illuminations of the Holy Spirit?

Second, I answer that men under the Gospel are entirely without excuse for not enjoying all the light they need from the Holy Spirit, since He is in the world and has been sent for the very purpose of giving to all the knowledge of themselves and of Christ that they need. His aid is freely offered to all, and Christ has assured us that the

Father is more willing to give the Holy Spirit to those who ask Him than parents are to give good gifts to their children (Luke 11:13).

All men under the Gospel know this, and all men have enough light to ask in faith for the Holy Spirit. And, of course, all men may know of themselves and of Christ all that they need to know. They are therefore able to know and to embrace Christ as fully and as fast as it is their duty to embrace Him. They are able to know Christ in His roles just as fast as they come into circumstances that require that they know Him in these various roles. The Holy Spirit, if He is not quenched and resisted, will surely reveal Christ in all His roles and fullness in due time, so that in every temptation a way of escape will be open so that we will be able to bear it. This is clearly promised:

> *No temptation has overtaken you except such as is common to man; but God is faithful, who will not allow you to be tempted beyond what you are able, but with the temptation will also make the way of escape, that you may be able to bear it.* (1 Corinthians 10:13)

People are able to know what God offers to teach them, for the condition of their learning is within the realm of their ability. The Holy Spirit offers, on the condition of faith in the plain promise of God, to lead every person into *"all truth"* (John 16:13). Every person is therefore under obligation to know and do the whole truth as far and as fast as it is possible for him to do so with the light of the Holy Spirit.

Chapter 9

Christle, Our Life

❖◆❖

When Christ who is our life appears, then you also
will appear with Him in glory.
—Colossians 3:4

Remember that it is not enough for us to see
Christ as the true God and the Eternal
Life, but we also need to lay hold of Him as
our Life. We must understand that a particular
and personal acceptance of Christ as our Life is
indispensable. Without it, we cannot be rooted
and grounded, established and perfected in love
(Ephesians 3:17). When our utter deficiency and
emptiness in any one aspect of our lives is deeply
revealed to us by the Holy Spirit, along with the
corresponding remedy and perfect fullness in
Christ, it then remains for the soul to cast off self
and to put on Christ. When this is done, when

self in that aspect is dead, and Christ is risen and lives and reigns in the heart in that role, all is strong, whole, and complete in that department of our lives and experience.

For example, suppose we find ourselves, because of our own selves or because of our circumstances, exposed to certain temptations that overcome us. Through this experience, we observe our weakness in a particular area. But after observing our susceptibility and tasting our weakness, suppose we begin piling resolution upon resolution. We bind ourselves with oaths and promises and covenants, but all in vain. When we resolve to stand, we invariably, in the presence of the temptation, fall.

This process of resolving and falling brings the soul into great discouragement and perplexity, until at last the Holy Spirit fully reveals to us that we are attempting to stand and to build on nothing. We clearly see the utter emptiness and uselessness of our resolutions and self-originated efforts. As a result, our self-dependence is forever annihilated in this aspect of our lives.

Now the soul is prepared for the revelation of Christ to meet this particular need. Christ is revealed and recognized as the soul's Substitute, Guarantee, Life, and Salvation in respect to the particular weakness that has been fully and disconcertingly revealed. Now, if the soul utterly and forever casts off and renounces self and puts on the Lord Jesus to meet its need, then all is complete in Him. To this extent Christ is reigning within us. To this extent we know the power of His resurrection and are conformed to His death (Philippians 3:10).

But I said that we need to know and to lay hold of Christ as *our* Life. We cannot put too much emphasis on our personal responsibility to Christ—our individual relationship to Him, our personal interest in Him, and our own obligation to Him. To sanctify our own souls, we need to make every department of faith a personal matter between us and God. We need to pay attention to every precept of the Bible, along with every promise, saying, exhortation, and warning. In short, we need to regard the whole Bible as given to us; we need to earnestly seek the personal revelation to our own souls of every truth it contains.

The Bible and all it contains is a message sent from heaven to us personally—a message that we need to bring home to our hearts. No one can understand this need too fully or feel it too deeply. No one can too earnestly desire the promised Spirit to teach him the true spiritual import of all the Bible's contents. The Bible must become a personal revelation of God to our own souls. It must become our own Book. We must know Christ for ourselves. We must know Him in His different roles. We must know Him in His blessed and infinite fullness. Otherwise, we cannot abide in Him, and unless we abide in Christ, we can bring forth none of the fruits of holiness. *"If anyone does not abide in Me, he is cast out as a branch and is withered"* (John 15:6).

In order to recognize and embrace Christ as our Life, we must understand that we in ourselves are *"dead in trespasses and sins"* (Ephesians 2:1). We have no life in ourselves. Death has reigned and will eternally reign in us and over us unless Christ becomes our Life.

Until a man knows that he is dead and that he is wholly destitute of spiritual life in himself, he will never know Christ as his Life. It is not enough to hold the *opinion* that all men are by nature *"dead in trespasses and sins."* It is not enough to have the opinion that we have this in common with all men and are dead in and of ourselves. We must *see* it. We must know what such language means. It must be made a matter of personal revelation to us. We must be made to fully recognize ourselves as dead and Christ as our Life. We must fully see ourselves as dead and Him as our Life by personally renouncing self in this respect and laying hold of Him as our own spiritual and eternal Life.

Many laypeople and, strange to say, some ministers—even prominent ministers—are so blinded that they suppose that an entirely sanctified soul no longer needs Christ. They assume that such a soul has spiritual life in and of itself, that it has some foundation or generator of continued holiness, as if the Holy Spirit had changed its nature and infused physical holiness or a holy principle into it.

When will such men—when will the church—understand that Christ is our Sanctification? We have no life, no holiness, no sanctification unless we abide in Christ and He in us. Apart from Christ, there is never any moral excellence in any man. When will the church realize this?

Furthermore, Christ does not change the physical makeup of man in sanctification; on the contrary, He only, by our own consent, gains and keeps the heart. He enthrones Himself, with our consent, in the heart, and through the heart He extends His influence and His life to our whole spiritual beings. He lives in us as truly as we live in our own bodies. He as truly reigns in our wills, and consequently in our emotions, by our own free consent, as our wills reign in our bodies. Entire sanctification is nothing else than the reign of Jesus in the soul. It is nothing more nor less than Christ, the Resurrection and the Life, raising the soul from spiritual death and reigning in it *through righteousness to eternal life* (Romans 5:21). When will the church realize these things?

Our All in All

We especially need to know Christ as the All in All. The Bible tells us that *"there is neither Greek nor Jew, circumcised nor uncircumcised, barbarian, Scythian, slave nor free, but Christ is all and in all"* (Colossians 3:11).

Before the soul can stop being overcome by temptation, it must renounce self-dependence in all things. It must be, as it were, self-annihilated. It must stop thinking of self as something that it can in any way rely on in the hour of trial. It must wholly and in all things renounce self and put on Christ. It must know self as nothing in the matter of spiritual life, and it must know Christ as All.

The psalmist could say, *"All my springs are in you"* (Psalm 87:7). Christ is the Fountain of Life. Whatever life there is in us flows directly from Him, even as the sap flows from the vine to the branch, or as a stream flows from its fountain. The spiritual life that is in us is really Christ's life flowing through us. Our activity, though properly our own, is nevertheless stimulated and directed by His presence and operation within us, so that we can and must say with Paul, *"It is no longer I who live, but Christ lives in me"* (Galatians 2:20).

It is a good thing for a conceited sinner to suffer, even in his own view, self-annihilation, as it relates to the origination of any spiritual obedience to God or any spiritual good what-soever. This must occur before he will learn to stand in Christ, to abide in Him as his All, on all occasions and in all things.

Oh, the infinite foolishness and madness of the carnal mind! It seems that it will always try its own strength before it will depend on Christ. It will first look for resources and help within itself before it will renounce self and make Christ its All in All. It will turn to its own wisdom, righteousness, sanctification, and redemption.

Sin has so fooled mankind that when Christ tells them *"without Me you can do nothing"* (John 15:5) and *"if anyone does not abide in Me, he is cast out as a branch and is withered"* (v. 6), they do not comprehend what He means or how much is really implied in these and similar sayings. However, one trial after another fully develops the appalling fact that they are nothing as far as spiritual good is concerned, and that Christ is *"all and in all"* (Colossians 3:11).

The Resurrection and the Life

Another role in which the soul must know Christ before it will steadily abide in Him is that of the Resurrection and the Life (John 11:25). Through and by Christ, the soul is raised from spiritual death. Christ, as the Resurrection and the Life, is raised in the soul. He raises or revives the divine image out of the spiritual death that reigns within us. He is begotten by the Holy Spirit and is born within us. He arises through the death that is within us and develops His own life within our own beings.

Are you saying, *"This is a hard saying; who can understand it?"* (John 6:60)? Until we know by our own experience the power of this resurrection within us, we will never understand *"the fellowship of His sufferings"* and be *"conformed to His death"* (Philippians 3:10). He raises our wills from their fallen state of death in trespasses and sins (Ephesians 2:1), or from their state of commitment and voluntary enslavement to lust and to self, to a state of conformity to the will of God. Through the intelligence, He pours a stream of quickening truth upon the soul. This is how He quickens the will into obedience. By making fresh revelations to the soul, He strengthens the will in obedience.

In this way, by raising, sustaining, and quickening the will, He corrects the sensibility—that department of the mind that feels, desires, suffers, and enjoys. He quickens and raises the whole man from the dead, or rather, builds up a new spiritual man upon the death and ruins of the old carnal man. He raises the same powers and faculties that were *"dead in trespasses and sins"* (Ephesians 2:1) to a spiritual life. He overcomes their death and inspires them with life. He lives in believers and works in them to will and to do (Philippians 2:13). And believers live in Him according to what Christ said in His address to His Father, *"As You, Father, are in Me, and I in You; that they also may be one in Us....I in them, and You in Me; that they may be made perfect in one"* (John 17:21, 23).

He does not raise the soul to spiritual life in any such sense that it has life separate from Him for one moment. The spiritual resurrection is a continual one. Christ is the Resurrection in the sense that He is at the foundation of all our obedience at every moment. He, as it were, raises the soul or the will from the slavery of lust to a conformity to the will of God, in every instance and at every moment of its consecration to the will of God. But He does this only upon the condition of our recognizing and embracing Him as our Resurrection and Life.

The Bridegroom or Husband

Another very precious and influential role of Christ in the matter of our sanctification is that of the Bridegroom or Husband of the soul. The individual soul needs to be married to Christ; it needs to enter this relationship personally by its own consent. We know that mere earthly and outward marriages are nothing but sin unless the hearts are married. True marriage is of the heart, and the outward ceremony is only a public profession of the union of the hearts.

All marriage may be regarded as a symbol of the union into which the spiritual soul enters with Christ. This relationship of Christ to the soul is frequently recognized both in the Old and the New Testament. It was treated by Paul as *"a great mystery"* (Ephesians 5:32).

The seventh and eighth chapters of Romans present a striking illustration of the results of the soul's remaining under the law on the one hand, and of its being married to Christ on the other. The seventh chapter begins as follows:

> *Or do you not know, brethren (for I speak to those who know the law), that the law has dominion over a man as long as he lives? For the woman who has a husband is bound by the law to her husband as long as he lives. But if the husband dies, she is released from the law of her husband. So then if, while her husband lives, she marries another man, she will be called an adulteress; but if her husband dies, she is free from that law, so that she is no adulteress, though she has married another man. Therefore, my brethren, you also have become dead to the law through the body of Christ, that you may be married to another; to Him who was raised from the dead, that we should bear fruit to God.* (Romans 7:1–4)

The apostle Paul then proceeded to show the results of these two marriages, or relationships, of the soul. He said of the soul, referring to when it was married to the law, *"For when we were in the flesh, the sinful passions which were aroused by the law were at work in our members to bear fruit to death"* (Romans 7:5). But he proceeded to describe the soul that is married to Christ: *"We have been delivered from the law, having died to what we were held by, so that we should serve in the newness of the Spirit and not in the oldness of the letter"* (v. 6).

The remaining part of this seventh chapter is an account of the soul's bondage while married to the law, of its efforts to please its husband, its continual failures, its deep conviction, its selfish efforts, its consciousness of failures, and its consequent self-condemnation and despondency. It is perfectly obvious, when we consider the apostle's allegory in this chapter, that he was portraying an experience with the law for the purpose of contrasting it with the experience of one who has attained to the true liberty of perfect love.

The eighth chapter of Romans shows the results of the marriage of the soul to Christ. The soul is delivered from its bondage to the law and from the power of the law of sin in its members. It *"bring[s] forth fruit unto God"* (Romans 7:4 KJV). Christ has succeeded in gaining the affections of the soul. What the law could not do, Christ has done, and the righteousness of the law is now fulfilled in the soul.

I will tell the story of Romans 7 and 8 in different words so that you might better understand it. The soul is married to the law and acknowledges her obligation to obey her husband. The husband requires perfect love toward God and man. This love is lacking; the soul is selfish. The husband is displeased, and he threatens her with death if she does not love.

She recognizes the reasonableness of both the requirement and the threat, and she resolves to fully obey. But because she is selfish, the command and the threat only increase the difficulty. All her efforts to obey are for selfish reasons. The husband is justly firm and imperative in his demands. The wife trembles and promises and resolves to obey, but all in vain. Her obedience is only feigned and outward; it is not love. She becomes disheartened and gives up in despair.

As the death sentence is about to be executed, Christ appears. He witnesses the dilemma. He reveres, honors, and loves the husband. He entirely approves his requirement and the course he has taken. He condemns the wife in most unqualified terms. Still He pities and loves her with a deep love.

He will consent to nothing that will appear to disapprove the claims or the course of her husband. The husband's uprightness must be openly acknowledged; he must not be dishonored. In fact, he must be magnified and made honorable (Isaiah 42:21 KJV). Still Christ pities the wife so much that He is willing to die as her Substitute. This He does, and the wife is regarded as dying in and by Him, her Substitute.

Now, the death of either the husband or wife means that the marriage covenant is dissolved. Moreover, the wife, in the person of her Substitute, has died under and to the law, her husband. Now she is at liberty to remarry. Christ rises from the dead. The striking and overpowering manifestation of Christ's selfless love in dying for her subdues her selfishness and wins her whole soul.

Now she finds that her selfishness or self-gratification is broken, and the righteousness of the law of love is fulfilled in her heart. The second Husband requires just what the first required, but since her whole heart has been won, she no longer needs to resolve to love, for love is as natural and spontaneous as her breath. Before, the seventh chapter of Romans was the language of her complaint. Now the eighth chapter is the language of her triumph. Before, she found herself unable to meet the demands of her husband, and equally unable to satisfy her own conscience. Now she finds it easy to obey her Husband. She discovers that *"His commandments are not burdensome"* (1

John 5:3), although they are identical with those of the first husband.

Now, Paul's allegory is not a mere rhetorical flourish. It represents a reality, one of the most important and glorious realities in existence, namely, the real spiritual union of the soul to Christ, and the blessed result of this union, which is the bringing forth of fruit unto God (Romans 7:4 KJV). This union is, as the apostle said, *"a great mystery"* (Ephesians 5:32); nevertheless, it is a glorious reality. *"He who is joined to the Lord is one spirit with Him"* (1 Corinthians 6:17).

Now, until the soul knows what it is to be married to the law and is able to adopt the language of the seventh chapter of Romans, it is not prepared to see and appreciate and be properly affected by the death and the love of Christ. Great multitudes rest in this first marriage; they do not consent to die and rise again in Christ. They are not married to Christ and do not know that there is such a thing; on the contrary, they expect to live and die in this bondage, crying out, *"O wretched man that I am!"* (Romans 7:24). They need to die and rise again in Christ to a new life founded in and growing out of a new relationship to Christ. Christ becomes the living Head or Husband of the soul, its Guarantee, its Life. He gains and retains the deepest affection of the soul, thus writing His law in the heart (Jeremiah 31:33) and engraving it in the innermost being.

Not only must the soul know what it is to be married to the law with its consequent bondage and death, but it must also enter for itself into the marriage relationship with a risen, living Christ. This must not be a theory, an opinion, a tenet; nor must it be an object of the imagination, a speculation, a notion, a dream. It must be a living, personal, real entering into a personal and living union with Christ, a most entire and universal giving of self to Him and receiving of Him in the role of spiritual Husband and Head. The Spirit of Christ and our spirits must embrace each other and enter into an everlasting covenant with each other. There must be a mutual giving of self and receiving of each other, a blending of spirits in such a sense as was intended by Paul in the passage already quoted: *"He who is joined to the Lord is one spirit with Him"* (1 Corinthians 6:17).

Chapter 10

Christus, Our Shepherd

———◇◆◇———

The LORD is my shepherd; I shall not want. He
makes me to lie down in green pastures; He leads me
beside the still waters.
—Psalm 23:1–2

A nother interesting and important relationship of Christ to His people is that of
Shepherd. Christians are helpless and defense-
less in this life without Christ's guardianship and
protection. Christ was revealed to the psalmist as
the Shepherd (see Psalm 23), and when He was
on earth, He revealed Himself to His disciples as
the Shepherd. (See John 10:11.)

It is not enough, however, that He be revealed
merely in words as our Shepherd. The real spiritual meaning of this needs to be revealed by

the Holy Spirit. The Spirit gives this truth power and produces a complete trust in the presence, care, and protection of Christ. This trust is often essential to preventing a fall in the hour of temptation.

Christ meant all that He said when He professed to be the Good Shepherd who cared for His sheep, who would not flee but would lay down His life for them. (See John 10:11–15.) In this role, as in all others, there is infinite fullness and perfection. If the sheep thoroughly know and confide in the shepherd, they will follow him, will flee to him for protection from every danger, will always depend on him for all things.

Now, all this is received and possessed in theory by all professing Christians. Yet how few seem to have had Christ revealed to them in such a way that they have actually embraced Him as their Shepherd and are continually depending on Him for all that a shepherd does. Now, either His being our Shepherd is a vain boast of Christ, or He may be and ought to be depended on. Either His being our Shepherd is false, or the soul has a right to throw itself on Him for all that is implied in the name *Good Shepherd*.

However, this role of Shepherd, along with all the other roles of Christ, implies that there is a corresponding need in us. We must see and feel this need, or this role of Christ will have no significance to us. In this case, then, as in all others, we need the revelation of the Holy Spirit. He will cause us to thoroughly comprehend our dependence on Christ. He will reveal Christ in the spirit and fullness of this role. And He will urge us to accept Christ as Shepherd until our souls have thoroughly done so.

Some fall into the mistake of supposing that when both their needs and the fullness of Christ have been revealed to the mind by the Spirit, the work is done. But unless they actually receive Him and commit themselves to Him as their Shepherd, they will soon find to their shame that nothing has been done to help them stand in the hour of temptation. Christ may be clearly revealed in any of His roles, the soul may see both its needs and His fullness, and yet the soul may forget or neglect to actively and personally receive Him in this role. It should never be forgotten that this is in every case indispensable. The revelation is designed to cause us to accept Him; if it does not do this, it has only greatly increased our guilt without at all increasing our benefits.

It is amazing to see how common it is and has been for ministers to overlook this truth. They have neither practiced it themselves nor urged it upon their hearers. Hence, Christ is not known to multitudes and is not in many cases received even when He is revealed by the Holy Spirit. If I am not mistaken, error upon this subject exists to a most appalling extent. The personal and individual acceptance of Christ in all His offices and roles is indispensable to entire sanctification. Yet it seems to me that this is seldom understood and insisted on by ministers today, and, of course, it is little thought of by the church. The idea of accepting for themselves a whole Savior, of taking hold of all the offices and roles of Jesus for their own individual selves, seems to be a rare idea to people in this age of the church. But knowing Christ this way is indispensable to securing our sanctification. If we know Him as Shepherd, we will follow Him, but not otherwise. Let this be well considered.

The Door

Christ is also the Door by which the soul enters the fold and finds security and protection among the sheep. This also needs to be spiritually understood, and the Door needs to be spiritually and personally entered to secure the guardianship of the Good Shepherd. Those who do not spiritually and truly see Christ as the Door and enter through Him, and yet hope for salvation, are surely attempting to climb up some other way and are therefore thieves and robbers. (See John 10:1, 7–9.)

This is a familiar and well-known truth, not only to every minister and Christian, but to every

Sunday school child. Yet how few really see and embrace its spiritual significance. That there is no other way to enter the fold of God is admitted by all who are orthodox. But who really perceives and knows through the personal revelation of the Holy Spirit all that Christ meant in the very significant words, *"Most assuredly, I say to you, I am the door of the sheep"* (John 10:7)? Who really understands His words, *"I am the door. If anyone enters by Me, he will be saved, and will go in and out and find pasture"* (v. 9)? He who truly discovers this Door and gains access by it will surely realize in his own experience the faithfulness of the Good Shepherd, and he *"will go in and out and find pasture."* That is, he will surely be fed; he will be led into green pastures and beside the still waters (Psalm 23:2).

But it is a good idea to ask what is implied in this role of Christ. That Christ is the Door implies the following:

1. We are shut out from the protection and favor of God unless we approach Him through and by Christ.

2. We need to know and clearly comprehend and appreciate this fact.

3. We need to discover the Door and what is implied both in the Door and in entering it. Entering it implies

the utter renunciation of self—of self-righteousness, self-protection, and self-support—and the putting of ourselves entirely under the control and protection of the Shepherd.

4. We need the revelation of the Holy Spirit to cause us to clearly understand the true spiritual significance of this role and what is implied in it.

5. When Christ is revealed in this role, we need to embrace Him. We need to enter for ourselves by and through Him into the enclosure that everywhere surrounds the children of God.

We need an inward revelation, not a mere outward revelation. Entering the sheepfold is an inward entering, a heart entering, and not a mere notion, idea, theory, or daydream. It is really an intelligent act of the mind. Entering the fold or favor of God through Christ is as real as entering the church on a Sunday through the door.

When the soul enters by the Door, it finds an entirely different reception and an entirely different treatment from that of those who climb up into the church on a ladder of mere opinion, a scaling ladder of mere orthodoxy. Those who do not enter through the Door are not fed. They find no protection from the Good Shepherd. They do not know the Shepherd and follow Him because they have climbed up another way. They do not have confidence in Him; they cannot approach Him with boldness and claim His guardianship and protection. Their knowledge of Christ is only an opinion, a theory, a heartless and fruitless speculation. Oh, how many give the saddest proof that they have never entered by the Door and, consequently, have no realization of the blessed protection and support of the Good Shepherd!

Here I must not forget to again insist on the necessity of a personal revelation of the nature of our relationship to God: we are excluded from all access to Him and His favor except through Christ the Door. Let this never for one moment be forgotten or overlooked. I must enter for and by myself. I must truly enter. I must be conscious that I enter. I must be sure that I do not misunderstand what is implied in entering. And, at my peril, I must not forget or neglect to enter.

The Way of Salvation

Christ is also the Way of Salvation. (See John 14:6.) Notice that He is not a mere teacher of the way, as some vainly imagine and teach. Christ is truly the Way itself. He Himself is the Way. Works are not the way, whether works of law or works of faith. Works of faith are a condition of salvation, but they are not the way. Faith is not the way.

Faith is a condition of entering and abiding in this way, but it is not the way. Christ Himself is the Way. Faith receives Him to reign in the soul and to be its salvation. But it is Christ Himself who is the Way. The soul is saved by Christ Himself— not by doctrine, not by the Holy Spirit, not by works of any kind, not by faith or love or anything whatsoever, but by Christ Himself.

The Holy Spirit reveals and introduces Christ to the soul, and the soul to Christ. He takes of what is Christ's and shows it to us (John 16:14). But He leaves it to Christ to save us. He urges and induces us to accept Christ, to receive Him by faith as He reveals Him to us. But Christ is the Way. It is His being received by us that saves the soul. But we must perceive the Way. We must enter this Way by our own act. We must proceed in this Way. We must continue in this Way to the end of life and to all eternity; these are indispensable conditions of our salvation.

"Where I go you know, and the way you know" (John 14:4), said Christ. Thomas said to Him, *"Lord, we do not know where You are going, and how can we know the way?"* (v. 5). Jesus replied,

> *I am the way, the truth, and the life. No one comes to the Father except through Me. If you had known Me, you would have known My Father also; and from now on you know Him and have seen Him.* (vv. 6–7)

Here Christ so identified Himself with the Father that He insisted that he who had seen one had seen the other. Therefore, when He said, *"No one comes to the Father except through Me,"* we are to understand that no one can expect to find the true God anywhere else but in Him. The visible Christ embodied the true Godhead (Colossians 2:9). He is the way to God because He is the true God and the Eternal Life and Salvation of the soul.

Many seem to understand Christ in this role as nothing more than a teacher of a system of morality, by the observance of which we may be saved. Others regard this role as only implying that He is the way in the sense of making an atonement and thus rendering it possible for us to be forgiven. Still others understand this language as implying not only that Christ made an atonement and opened up a way of access to God through His death and mediation, but also that He teaches us the great truths essential to our salvation.

Now, all this, in my understanding, falls infinitely short of the true spiritual meaning of Christ and the true spiritual significance of His role as the Way. Beyond question, these things are implied and included in this role, but they are not the whole truth nor the essential truth intended in this declaration of Christ's. He did not say, "I came to open the way," "I came to teach the way," or "I came to call you into the way," but *"I am the way"* (John 14:6).

Suppose He had meant merely that His instructions pointed out the way, or that His death was to open the way and His teaching point it out. Would He not have said, "What! Have I taught you so long, and yet you have not understood My doctrine?" instead of saying, *"Have I been with you so long, and yet you have not known Me"* (v. 9)? Would He not have said, "I have taught you the way," instead of saying, *"I am the way"* (v. 6)? The fact is, there is a meaning in these words more profoundly spiritual than His disciples then and many now seem capable of understanding. He Himself is the Way of Salvation because He is the salvation of the soul. He is the way to the Father because He is in the Father and the Father is in Him (v. 10). He is the way to eternal life because He Himself is the very essence and substance of eternal life. The soul that finds Him does not need to look for eternal life, for it has found it already.

The questions of Thomas and Philip in the John 14 passage show how little they really knew of Christ before they received the baptism of the Holy Spirit. Similarly, vast multitudes of today's professing disciples do not seem to know Christ as the Way. They do not seem to know Christ in this role as He is revealed by the Holy Spirit. The Comforter's revelation of Christ as the Way is indispensable to our knowing Him so well that we are able to stand in the hour of temptation. We must enter and walk in and abide in this True and Living Way for ourselves. It is a Living Way and not a mere speculation.

Do you know Christ by the Holy Spirit as the Living Way? Do you know Christ as a personal acquaintance? Or do you know Him only by report, by hearsay, by preaching, by reading, and by study? Do you know Him as in the Father and the Father as in Him (John 14:10)? Philip seemed not to have had a personal, spiritual revelation to his own soul of the deity of Christ. (See John 14:8–9.) Have you had this revelation? And when He has been revealed to you as the True and Living Way, have you by faith personally entered the Way? Do you abide steadfastly in it? Do you know by experience what it means to live and move and have your very being in God (Acts 17:28)?

Do not be deceived. He who does not spiritually discern and enter the Way, he who does not abide in it to the end, cannot be saved. See to it, then, that you know the way to be saved, to be justified, to be sanctified. See to it that you do not mistake the way and take some other way. Remember, works are not the way. Faith is not the way. Doctrine is not the way. All these are conditions of salvation, but *Christ in His own person is the Way*. His own life living in and united to you is the Way and the only Way. You enter this Way by faith. Works of faith result from and are a condition of abiding in this Way, but the Way itself is the indwelling, living, personally embraced Christ, the *"true God and eternal life"* (1 John 5:20).

Amen, Lord Jesus. The Way is pleasant, and all its paths are peace (Proverbs 3:17).

The Truth

Christ is also the Truth (John 14:6). We must see Him and embrace Him as the Truth so that we will not fall in the hour of trial. Many know Christ merely as one who declared the truth, as one who revealed the true God and the way of salvation. This is all they understand by Christ's assertion that He is the Truth.

But if this is all, why may we not say the same thing with equal truth about Moses, about Paul, and about John? They taught the truth. They revealed the true God as far as holy lives and true doctrine are concerned. Yet who ever heard of Moses, Paul, or John as being the way or the truth? Although they taught the way and the truth, they were neither the way nor the truth. But Christ is the Truth.

What, then, is truth? Why, Christ is the Truth. Whoever spiritually knows Christ knows the truth. Words are not the truth. Ideas are not the truth. Both words and ideas may be signs or representations of the truth. But the truth has a being and a home in Christ. He is the embodiment and the essence of truth. He is reality. He is substance and not shadow. (See Colossians 2:16–17.) He is truth revealed. He is essential, eternal, immutable, necessary, absolute, self-existent, infinite Truth. When the Holy Spirit reveals truth, He reveals Christ. When Christ reveals truth, He reveals Himself.

Philosophers have found it difficult to define truth. Pilate asked Christ, *"What is truth?"* (John 18:38) but did not wait for an answer. The term is undoubtedly used in a double sense. Sometimes the mere reflection or representation of things in signs—such as words, actions, writings, pictures, diagrams, and so on—is called truth, and this is the common understanding of the word. But all things that exist are only signs, reflections, symbols, representations, or types of the Author of all things. That is, the universe is only the objective representation of the subjective truth, or is the reflection or reflector of God. It is the mirror that reflects the essential Truth, or the true and living God.

I am aware that no one but the Holy Spirit can persuade the mind of the significance of Christ's assertion that He is the Truth. It is full of mystery and darkness. It is only a figure of speech to the person who has not been enlightened by the Holy Spirit concerning its true spiritual significance.

The Holy Spirit does not reveal all the roles of Christ to the soul at once. Hence, there are many to whom Christ has been revealed in some of His roles while other roles are still veiled from view. Each distinct name and office and role needs to be made the subject of a special and personal revelation to the soul, both to meet its needs and to strengthen it in obedience under all circumstances.

Christ must be revealed and comprehended as the essential, eternal, immutable Truth, and the soul must embrace Him as such. All that is commonly called truth is only a reflection of Him. When the mind comprehends Him as the Truth, it finds a rock, a resting place, a foundation, a stability, a reality, a power that it had no conception of before.

If this is unintelligible to you, I cannot help it. The Holy Spirit can explain and make you see it; I cannot. Christ is not truth in the sense of mere doctrine, nor in the sense of a teacher of true doctrine, but as the substance or essence of truth. He is that which all doctrinal truth describes. True doctrine describes Him but is not identical with Him. Truth in doctrine is only the sign, the declaration, the representation of truth—of living, absolute, self-existent truth in the Godhead.

Truth in doctrine or true doctrine is a medium through which substantial or essential truth is revealed. But the doctrine or medium is no more identical with truth than light is identical with the objects that it reveals. Truth in doctrine is called light, and it is to essential truth what light is to the objects that reflect it. Light reflecting from objects is at once the condition of and the medium for revealing them. Likewise, true doctrine is the condition and the means of knowing Christ, the essential Truth. All truth in doctrine is only a reflection of Christ, or it is an enlightening of the intelligence by Christ.

When we learn this spiritually, we will learn to distinguish between doctrine and the One whose radiance it is. We will learn to worship Christ as the Truth and not the doctrine that reveals Him. We will learn to worship God instead of the Bible. We will then find our way through the shadow to the substance. Many, no doubt, make the mistake of falling down and worshiping the doctrine, the preacher, the Bible, the shadow, and do not look for the unspeakably glorious substance, of which this bright and sparkling truth is only the sweet and mild reflection.

The True Light

While in the above illustration, Christ is represented as the object that is reflected by the light, there is a very real sense in which Christ is the Light. In fact, more than once the Bible refers to Christ as the Light. John said that Christ is *"the true Light which gives light to every man coming into the world"* (John 1:9). He also said, *"In Him was life, and the life was the light of men. And the light shines in the darkness, and the darkness did not comprehend it"* (vv. 4–5).

What is the source of spiritual light? The Bible says Christ is. But what does this mean? When it is said that He is the true Light, does it mean only that He is the teacher of true doctrine? No, it means that He is the Light in which true doctrine is comprehended. He shines through and upon all spiritual doctrine and causes its spiritual significance to be grasped. The presence of His light, or, in other words, His own presence, is a condition of any doctrine's being spiritually understood.

Christ is no doubt the essential Light; that is, light is an attribute of His divinity. Essential, uncreated light is one of the attributes of Christ as God. It is a spiritual attribute, of course, but it is an essential and natural attribute of Christ. Whoever knows Christ after the Spirit—whoever has a true, spiritual, and personal acquaintance with Christ as God—knows that Christ *is* light.

The Bible says that He covers Himself *"with light as with a garment"* (Psalm 104:2). He illuminates the heavenly world with such an indescribable light that no man can approach it and live. (See 1 Timothy 6:16.) The strongest seraphim are unable to look with unveiled face upon His overpowering brilliance. To a spiritual mind, these are not mere figures of speech. They are understood by those who walk in the light of Christ to mean what they say.

I dwell upon this particular role of Christ because of the importance of its being understood. Christ is the real and true Light who alone can cause us to see spiritual things as they are. Without His light, we walk in the midst of the most overpowering realities without being aware of them at all. As one deprived of natural light gropes his way and does not know at what he stumbles, so one deprived of the presence of the light of Christ gropes his way and does not know at what he stumbles. To attain to true spiritual illumination and to continue to walk in this light is indispensable to entire sanctification.

Oh, that this were understood! Christ must be known as the true and only Light of the soul. This must not be held merely as a tenet; it must be understood, spiritually examined, and known.

That Christ is in some undetermined sense the Light of the soul and the true Light is generally admitted, just as multitudes of other things are admitted without being at all spiritually and experientially understood. But this role or attribute of Christ must be spiritually known by experience as a condition of abiding in Him.

John said,

> *This is the message which we have heard from Him...that God is light and in Him is no darkness at all. If we say that we have fellowship with Him, and walk in darkness, we lie and do not practice the truth. But if we walk in the light as He is in the light, we have fellowship with one another, and the blood of Jesus Christ His Son cleanses us from all sin.*
>
> (1 John 1:5–8)

This Light has come into the world. If men do not love darkness rather than light (John 3:19), they will know Christ as the true Light of the soul and will walk in the light and not stumble.

Christ within Us

There is another role of Christ in the life of a believer, and it is indispensable that the believer recognize and spiritually understand it in order to be entirely sanctified. It is Christ within us.

"Do you not know yourselves," said the apostle Paul, *"that Jesus Christ is in you?; unless indeed you are disqualified"* (2 Corinthians 13:5). Paul had more to say on this subject:

> But you are not in the flesh but in the Spirit, if indeed the Spirit of God dwells in you. Now if anyone does not have the Spirit of Christ, he is not His. And if Christ is in you, the body is dead because of sin, but the Spirit is life because of righteousness.   (Romans 8:9–10)

> My little children, for whom I labor in birth again until Christ is formed in you.
>   (Galatians 4:19)

> It is no longer I who live, but Christ lives in me.
>   (Galatians 2:20)

Many know Christ only as an outward Christ, as One who lived many centuries ago, who died, arose, and ascended on high, and who now lives in heaven. They read all this in the Bible, and in a certain sense they believe it. That is, they admit it to be true historically. But do they have Christ risen within them? This is quite another thing. Christ in heaven making intercession is one thing; this is a great and glorious truth. But Christ in the soul, also living there to make *"intercession for us with groanings which cannot be uttered"* (Romans 8:26), is another thing.

The Spirit who dwells in believers is frequently represented in the Bible as the Spirit of Christ and as Christ Himself. Thus, in the passage just quoted from the eighth chapter of Romans, the apostle Paul represented the Spirit of God who dwells in believers as the Spirit of Christ and as Christ Himself. Let us look at this passage again:

> *But you are not in the flesh but in the Spirit, if indeed the Spirit of God dwells in you. Now if anyone does not have the Spirit of Christ, he is not His. And if Christ is in you, the body is dead because of sin, but the Spirit is life because of righteousness.* (Romans 8:9–10)

This concept is common in the Bible. The Spirit of Christ, then, or the real deity of Christ, dwells in the truly spiritual believer.

However, this fact needs to be spiritually understood and kept distinctly and continually in view. Christ not only in heaven but within us, as truly inhabiting our bodies as we do, as really in us as we are in ourselves, is the teaching of the Bible. This teaching must be spiritually understood by a divine, personal, and inward revelation in order to secure our abiding in Him.

Not only do we need the real presence of Christ within us, but we need His manifested presence to sustain us in hours of conflict. Christ may be as present inside us as He is outside us without our recognizing His presence. He has made His manifesting Himself *with* and *in* us contingent on our faith and obedience.

When Christ manifests Himself within us, we are assured of His constant and real presence. In this way, He establishes and strengthens the confidence and obedience of the soul. To know Christ *"according to the flesh"* (2 Corinthians 5:16), or merely historically as an outward Savior, is of no spiritual help. We must know Him as an inward Savior, as Jesus risen and reigning in us, as having arisen and established His throne in our hearts, and as having written and established the authority of His law there. The *"old man"* dethroned and crucified (Romans 6:6), Christ risen within us and united to us in such a sense that we are *"one spirit with Him"* (1 Corinthians 6:17)—this is the only condition and secret of entire sanctification.

Oh, that this were understood! Why, many ministers talk and write about sanctification as if they suppose that it consists of and results from a mere self-originated formation of holy habits. What infinite blindness! True sanctification consists of entire consecration to God; however, may it ever be remembered that this consecration is induced and perpetuated by the Spirit of Christ.

The fact that Christ is in us needs to be so clearly understood that it annihilates the idea that Christ is only far off in heaven. The soul needs to so grasp this truth that it turns within and does not look without for Christ, that it naturally seeks communion with Him in the closet of the soul, or within, and does not let the thoughts go in search of Him without.

Christ made the following promises: to come and take up His abode with His people (John 14:23), to manifest Himself to them (v. 21), to send His own Spirit to abide with them forever (v. 16), to be with them and in them (v. 17). Now, all this needs to be spiritually understood. We need to recognize that Christ by His Spirit is as present with us as we are with ourselves, is as near to us as we are to ourselves, and is infinitely more interested in us than we are in ourselves.

This spiritual recognition of Christ present with and in us has an overpowering delight in it. The soul rests in Him and lives, walks, and has its being in His light. It drinks at the fountain of His love and from the river of His pleasures (Psalm 36:8). It enjoys His peace and leans on His strength.

Chapter 11

Christy, Our Strength

———◆———◆———◆———

*To You, O my Strength, I will sing praises; for God is
my defense, my God of mercy.*
—Psalm 59:17

We must also spiritually know Christ as our
Strength as a condition of entire sanctification. The psalmist referred to God as his
strength many times: *"I will love You, O LORD,
my strength"* (Psalm 18:1); *"O LORD, my strength"*
(Psalm 19:14); *"Pull me out of the net…for You
are my strength"* (Psalm 31:4); *"You are the God of
my strength"* (Psalm 43:2); *"Blessed be the LORD my
strength"* (Psalm 144:1 KJV). In Isaiah 27:5, the
Lord says, *"Let him take hold of My strength, that
he may make peace with Me."* Jeremiah said, *"O
LORD, my strength"* (Jeremiah 16:19). In Habakkuk
3:19, we read, *"God is my strength."* Christ said

to Paul, *"My strength is made perfect in weakness"* (2 Corinthians 12:9). We are commanded to *"be strong in the Lord and in the power of His might"* (Ephesians 6:10), that is, to lay hold of His strength by faith. As we read in Isaiah 27:5, we are exhorted to take hold of His strength as a condition of making peace with God.

That God is in some sense our Strength is generally admitted. But I fear it is rare for people to understand the true spiritual sense in which He is our Strength. Many take refuge, not in His strength by faith, but in the plea that He is their strength and that they have none of their own; meanwhile, they continue in sin. They neither truly understand nor believe that God is their strength. With all who say that God is their strength and yet live in sin, this statement is an opinion, a tenet, a saying, but by no means a spiritually understood and embraced truth. If the real meaning of this language were spiritually understood and embraced with the heart, the soul would no longer live in sin. It would not be overcome by temptation while laying hold of Christ any more than God would be overcome.

The conditions of spiritually understanding Christ as our Strength are as follows:

1. The spiritual understanding of our own weakness, both its nature and degree

2. The revelation to us of Christ as our
    Strength by the Holy Spirit

When these revelations are truly made and
self-dependence is therefore forever annihilated,
the soul comes to understand wherein its strength
lies. It renounces forever its own strength and
relies wholly on the strength of Christ. It does
not do this in the sit-still, do-nothing sense of the
term; on the contrary, it actively takes hold of
Christ's strength and uses it in doing the entire
will of God. It takes hold of Christ's strength and
goes about producing every good word and work.
It holds on to and leans on Christ as a helpless
man would lean on the arm or shoulder of a
strong man for assistance in going about doing
good.

This is not a state of quietism. This is not
a mere opinion, a sentiment, a sham. With the
sanctified soul, one of the clearest realities in
existence is that he leans on and uses the strength
of Christ. He knows himself to be constantly and
perseveringly active in availing himself of the
strength of Christ. Since he is perfectly weak in
himself or perfectly emptied of his own strength,
Christ's strength is made perfect in his weakness
(2 Corinthians 12:9).

When a person renounces his own strength,
he is not denying his natural ability in the sense
that he is charging God with requiring what he

is unable to perform. He is completely recognizing his ability were he inclined to do all that God requires of him, and he thoroughly and honestly condemns himself for not using his powers as God requires. But while he recognizes his natural liberty or ability and his consequent obligation, at the same time he clearly and spiritually sees that he has been too long the slave of lust to ever assert or to maintain his spiritual supremacy as the master instead of the slave of appetite. Clearly and pitifully, the will or heart is so weak in the presence of temptation that there is no hope of its maintaining its integrity unsupported by strength from Christ. Therefore, it renounces forever its dependence on its own strength and casts itself wholly and forever on the strength of Christ.

Christ's strength is obtained only on the condition of fully renouncing one's own. And Christ's strength is made perfect in the soul of man only in its entire weakness, that is, only in the absence of all dependence on its own strength. Self must be renounced in every respect in which we lay hold of Christ. He will not share the throne of the heart with us, nor will He be put on by us except to the extent that we put off ourselves. (See Ephesians 4:22; Galatians 3:27.) Lay aside all dependence on yourself in every respect in which you want Christ. Many reject Christ by depending on self, and they seem not to be aware of their error.

Now, let it be understood and constantly kept in mind that this self-renunciation and taking hold of Christ as our Strength is not merely a speculation, an opinion, an article of faith, or a profession. It must be one of the most practical realities in the world. It must become to your mind an ever present reality. When it does, you will not attempt anything in your own strength any more than a man who has never walked without crutches would attempt to rise and walk on his own. To such a man, his crutches become a part of him. They are his legs. He uses them as naturally as we use the members of our bodies. He does not forget them or try to walk without them any more than we attempt to walk without our feet.

Now, it is the same way with one who spiritually understands his dependence on Christ. He knows he can walk and that he must walk, but he as naturally uses the strength of Christ in all his duties as the lame man uses his crutches. It is as truly an ever present reality to him that he must lean on Christ as it is to the lame man that he must lean on his crutches. He learns on all occasions to keep hold of the strength of Christ and does not even think of doing anything without Him. He knows that he does not need to attempt anything in his own strength; he is aware that any such attempt would result in failure and disgrace just as surely as the lame man knows that for him to try to walk without his crutches would result in a fall.

This is a great lesson, and I fear it is a rarely learned lesson with professing Christians. Yet how strange that this is the case, since, in every instance since the world began, attempts to walk without Christ have resulted in complete and instantaneous failure. All profess to know their own weakness and their remedy, yet how few give evidence of knowing either.

Our Keeper

Christ is also the Keeper of the soul. In this role He must be revealed to and embraced by each soul as the condition of its abiding in Christ, or as a condition of entire sanctification, which is the same thing.

> *I will lift up my eyes to the hills; from whence comes my help? My help comes from the LORD, who made heaven and earth. He will not allow your foot to be moved; He who keeps you will not slumber. Behold, He who keeps Israel shall neither slumber nor sleep. The LORD is your keeper; the LORD is your shade at your right hand. The sun shall not strike you by day, nor the moon by night. The LORD shall preserve you from all evil; He shall preserve your soul. The LORD shall preserve your going out and your coming in from this time forth, and even forevermore.* (Psalm 121:1–8)

This psalm, along with many other passages of Scripture, depicts God as exerting an effective influence in preserving the soul from falling. Of course, He does not exert this influence physically or by compulsion, but it is and must be a moral influence, that is, an influence entirely consistent with our own free agency. But it is effective in the sense of being a prevailing influence.

However, in this role, as in all others, Christ must be seen and embraced. The soul must see and well appreciate its dependence in this respect and commit itself to Christ in this role. It must cease from its own works and from expecting to keep itself and must commit itself to Christ and abide in this state of commitment.

Keeping the soul implies watching over it to guard it against being overcome by temptation. This is exactly what the Christian needs. His enemies are the world, the flesh, and the devil. He has been enslaved by these. He has been consecrated to these. In their presence he is all weakness in himself. He needs a Keeper to accompany him, just as a reformed alcoholic sometimes needs someone to accompany and strengthen him in places of temptation. The long-established habits of the drunkard render him weak in the presence of his enemy, intoxicating liquor. Likewise, the Christian's long-cherished habits of self-indulgence render him all weakness and irresolution if left to himself in the presence of excited appetite or passion. As the alcoholic needs a friend and brother to warn him and to reason with him to strengthen his purposes, so the sinner needs the Comforter to warn him and to reason with him to sustain his fainting resolutions.

Christ has promised to do this. However, this promise, like all the promises, depends on our putting it to our own use by faith. Let us always, then, keep in mind the following condition of entire sanctification: the Lord must be spiritually seen and sincerely embraced and depended on as our Keeper. This must not be a mere opinion. It must be a thorough and honest uniting with Christ in this role.

A Friend

The soul needs to know Christ not merely as a master, but as a Friend.

> *Greater love has no one than this, than to lay down one's life for his friends. You are My friends if you do whatever I command you. No longer do I call you servants, for a servant does not know what his master is doing; but I have called you friends, for all things that I heard from My Father I have made known to you.*
> (John 15:13–15)

Jesus Christ took the utmost pains to inspire His disciples with the most implicit confidence in

Him. He does the same for us. Most Christians do not seem to have comprehended the humble condescension of Christ enough to appreciate fully, or even at all, His sincere regard for them. They seem afraid to regard Him in the light of a friend. They do not realize that they may approach Him on all occasions with the utmost confidence and holy familiarity. They do not know that He takes an active interest in everything that concerns them. They are unaware that He sympathizes with them in all their trials and cares more tenderly about them than we do for our dearest earthly friends.

Observe the emphasis that Christ gives to the strength of His friendship: He lays down His life for His friends. Now, imagine that you have an earthly friend who loves you so much that he would lay down his life for you, that he would die for a crime that you had committed against him. If you were assured of the strength of his friendship, and if you knew that his ability to help you in all circumstances was absolutely unlimited, with what confidence you would confide in him! How you would rest in his friendship and protection!

Even Christians are slow to see Christ in the role of their Friend. They stand in so much awe of Him that they fear to bring home to their hearts the full significance and reality of the friendship of Christ. Yet Christ takes the greatest pains to inspire them with the fullest confidence in His undying and most exalted friendship.

I have often thought that many professing Christians have never really and spiritually understood Christ in this role. This accounts for their depending on Him so little in seasons of trial. They do not realize that He truly feels for and sympathizes with them. His feelings for and sympathy with them, His deep interest in and pity for them—they do not spiritually see these as a reality. Hence, they stand aloof, or they approach Him only in words. At most, they come to Him with deep feeling and desire, but not in the unwavering confidence that they will receive the things that they ask of Him. However, if they want to prevail, they must believe.

> *Ask in faith, with no doubting, for he who doubts is like a wave of the sea driven and tossed by the wind. For let not that man suppose that he will receive anything from the Lord.*
> (James 1:6–7)

Christ's real, deep, and abiding affection for us, and His undying interest in us personally, must come to be a living and ever present reality to our souls. This will secure our own abiding in faith and love in all circumstances. There is perhaps no role of Christ in which we need to know Him more thoroughly than this one.

The friendship of Christ is admitted in words by almost everybody, yet it is realized and believed by almost nobody. How infinitely strange that Christ should have given such high evidence of His love and friendship for us, and that we should be so slow of heart to realize and believe it! But until this truth is really and spiritually understood and embraced, the soul will find it impossible to fly to Him in seasons of trial with implicit confidence in His favor. It will not see Him as our Friend who has laid down His life for us and would not hesitate to do it again, were it necessary. Yet it is a fact that our confidence in Him will secure our abiding in Him.

An Older Brother

Christ is also to be regarded and embraced as our older Brother. The following passages and others present Christ in the role of a brother.

For it was fitting for [God], *for whom are all things and by whom are all things, in bringing many sons to glory, to make the captain of their salvation perfect through sufferings. For both He who sanctifies and those who are being sanctified are all of one, for which reason He is not ashamed to call them brethren, saying: "I will declare Your name to My brethren; in the midst of the assembly I will sing praise to You." And again: "I will put My trust in Him." And again: "Here am I and the children whom God has given Me." Inasmuch then as the children have partaken of flesh and blood, He Himself likewise shared in the same, that through death He might destroy him who had the power of death, that is, the devil, and release those who through fear of death were all their lifetime subject to bondage. For indeed He does not give aid to angels, but He does give aid to the seed of Abraham. Therefore, in all things He had to be made like His brethren, that He might be a merciful and faithful High Priest in things pertaining to God, to make propitiation for the sins of the people. For in that He Himself has suffered, being tempted, He is able to aid those who are tempted.* (Hebrews 2:10–18)

Then Jesus said to them, "Do not be afraid. Go and tell My brethren to go to Galilee, and there they will see me." (Matthew 28:10)

Jesus said to her, "Do not cling to Me, for I have not yet ascended to My Father; but go to My brethren and say to them, 'I am ascending to My Father and your Father, and to My God and your God.'" (John 20:17)

For whom He foreknew, He also predestined to be conformed to the image of His Son, that He might be the firstborn among many brethren. (Romans 8:29)

So He is not merely our Friend, but our Brother. He is a brother possessing the attributes of God. Is it not of great importance that we should know Him and embrace Him as our Brother? It would seem as if He took all possible pains to inspire us with the most implicit confidence in Him. He is not ashamed to call us brothers. Should we refuse or neglect to embrace Him as our Brother and to avail ourselves of all that this means?

I have often thought that many professing Christians really regard the roles of Christ as existing only in name and not at all in reality and fact. "Am I not a man and a brother?" Christ says to the desponding and tempted soul. He Himself has said, *"A brother is born for adversity"* (Proverbs 17:17). He is the firstborn among many brothers, yet we are to be heirs with Him, heirs of God and joint heirs with Him of all the infinite riches of the Godhead (Romans 8:17).

We are *"foolish ones, and slow of heart"* (Luke 24:25) not to believe and receive this Brother to our wholehearted and eternal confidence. He must be spiritually revealed, seen, and embraced as our Brother if we are to experience His brotherly truthfulness.

The True Vine

Christ is the true Vine, and we are the branches (John 15:5). Do we know Him in this role, as our original source, as the fountain from which we receive our moment-by-moment nourishment and life? This union between Christ and our souls is formed by implicit faith in Him. By faith the soul leans on Him, feeds on Him, and receives a constantly sustaining influence from Him.

> *I am the true vine, and My Father is the vine-dresser. Every branch in Me that does not bear fruit He takes away; and every branch that bears fruit He prunes, that it may bear more fruit. You are already clean because of the word which I have spoken to you. Abide in Me, and I in you. As the branch cannot bear fruit of itself, unless it abides in the vine, neither can you, unless you abide in Me. I am the vine, you are the branches. He who abides in Me, and I in him, bears much fruit; for without Me you can do nothing. If anyone does not abide in Me, he is cast out as a branch and is withered; and they gather them and throw them into the fire, and they are burned. If you abide in Me, and My words abide in you, you will ask what you desire, and it shall be done for you. By this My Father is glorified, that you bear much fruit; so you will be My disciples.* (John 15:1–8)

Now, it is important for us to understand what it means to be in Christ in the sense of this passage. It certainly means to be so united to Him that we receive spiritual support and nourishment from Him. This spiritual nourishment is as real and as constant as the natural nourishment that the branch receives from the vine. *"If anyone does not abide in Me,"* Christ says, *"he is cast out as a branch and is withered"* (John 15:6).

Now, to abide in Him implies a union that keeps us spiritually alive and fresh. There are many professing Christians in the church who are withered. They do not abide in Christ. Their religion is stale. They can speak of former experiences, they can tell how they once knew Christ, but every spiritual mind can see that they are branches that have fallen off. They have no fruit. Their leaves are withered, their bark is dried, and they are fit only to be gathered and cast into the fire.

Oh, this stale, last-year's religion! Why will professing Christians who live on old experiences not understand that they are cast-off branches? Their withered, fruitless, lifeless, loveless, faithless, powerless condition testifies to their faces and to all men that they are fuel fit for the flames.

It is also of infinite importance that we know and spiritually understand the conditions of abiding in Christ in the relationship of a branch to a vine. We must recognize our various needs and

His infinite fullness and lay hold of all that is implied in these roles of Christ as quickly as Christ is revealed. In this way, we will abide in Him and receive all the spiritual nourishment that we need. But unless we are thus taught by the Spirit, and unless we thus believe, we will not abide in Him, nor will He abide in us.

If we do abide in Him, He says we will bear *"much fruit"* (John 15:5). *"Much fruit,"* then, is evidence that we do abide in Him, and fruitlessness is absolute evidence that we do not abide in Him. *"If you abide in Me, and My words abide in you, you will ask what you desire, and it shall be done for you"* (v. 7). Great effectiveness in prayer, then, is evidence that we abide in Him. But a lack of effectiveness in prayer is conclusive evidence that we do not abide in Him. In addition, no man sins while he properly abides in Christ. *"If anyone is in Christ, he is a new creation; old things have passed away; behold, all things have become new"* (2 Corinthians 5:17).

However, let it not be forgotten that we have to do something in order to abide in Christ. *"Abide in Me"* (John 15:4), says Christ; this is required of us. We do not begin the relationship of a branch to the Vine without our own activity, nor do we abide in Christ without a constant cleaving to Him by faith. Of necessity, the will must always be alive. It must cleave either to Christ or to something else. It is one thing to have this relationship in theory and an entirely different thing to understand it spiritually and to truly cleave to Christ as our constant fountain of spiritual life.

Chapter 12

Christ, the Fountain

❖

The LORD, the fountain of living waters.
—Jeremiah 17:13

Christ is also the *"fountain...opened for the house of David...for sin and for uncleanness"* (Zechariah 13:1). Let it ever be remembered and spiritually understood and embraced that Christ is not only a justifying Savior, but also a purifying Savior. His name is Jesus because He saves His people from their sins (Matthew 1:21).

Jesus

As Jesus, therefore, He must be spiritually known and embraced. Jesus, Savior! We are informed that He is called Jesus, or Savior, because He saves His people, not only from hell, but also from their sins. He saves from hell only on the condition of His saving from sin. A person has no Savior if he is not, in his experience, saved from sin. Of what use is it to call Jesus Lord and Savior unless He is truly, in a practical way, acknowledged as our Lord and as our Savior from sin? Will we call Him, "Lord, Lord," and not do the things that He says (Luke 6:46)? Will we call Him Savior and refuse to embrace Him in such a way that we are saved from our sins?

The One Who Cleanses from All Sin

We must know Him as the One whose blood cleanses us from all sin. We have many Scriptures that speak of this:

How much more shall the blood of Christ, who through the eternal Spirit offered Himself without spot to God, cleanse your conscience from dead works to serve the living God?
(Hebrews 9:14)

Knowing that you were not redeemed with corruptible things...but with the precious blood of Christ, as of a lamb without blemish and without spot. (1 Peter 1:18–19)

Elect according to the foreknowledge of God the Father, in sanctification of the Spirit, for obedience and sprinkling of the blood of Jesus Christ.
(v. 2)

*To Him who loved us and washed us from our
sins in His own blood.*   (Revelation 1:5)

When the shedding of Christ's blood is rightly
perceived and embraced, when His atonement
is correctly understood and received by faith, it
cleanses the soul from all sin. Or, I should say,
when Christ is received as the One who cleanses
us from sin by His blood, we will know what
James B. Taylor meant when he said, "I have
been into the fountain and am clean," and what
Christ meant when He said, *"You are already clean
because of the word which I have spoken to you"* (John
15:3).

Ezekiel 36:25–26 also speaks of our cleansing:

*Then I will sprinkle clean water on you, and
you shall be clean; I will cleanse you from all
your filthiness and from all your idols. I will
give you a new heart and put a new spirit
within you; I will take the heart of stone out of
your flesh and give you a heart of flesh.*

Christ must truly be revealed as the One who
cleanses from sin. It is of the greatest importance
that language like this, relating to our being
cleansed from sin by Christ, should be explained
to our souls by the Holy Spirit and embraced by
faith. Nothing but this can save us from sin. But
this will fully and effectively do the work. This

will cleanse us from *all* sin. This will cleanse us from all our filthiness and from all our idols. This will make us completely clean.

Wonderful

"His name will be called Wonderful" (Isaiah 9:6). No exclamation has been more common to me in the past few years than "Wonderful!" When contemplating the nature, the character, the offices, the roles, the salvation of Christ, I find myself either audibly or mentally exclaiming, "Wonderful!" My soul is filled with wonder, love, and praise as I am led by the Holy Spirit to understand Christ, sometimes in one and sometimes in another role, depending on my circumstances and trials.

From year to year, I am more and more *"astonished at the doctrine of the Lord"* (Acts 13:12 KJV) and at the Lord Himself. I have come to the conclusion that there is no end to this either in time or in eternity. No doubt, through all eternity Christ will continue to make revelations of Himself to His intelligent creatures that will cause them to exclaim, "Wonderful!" I find my wonder more and more excited from one stage of Christian experience to another.

Christ is indeed wonderful, contemplated from every point of view—as God, as Man, as God-man, as Mediator. Indeed, I hardly know in which of His many roles He appears most wonderful when one of His roles is revealed to me by the Holy Spirit. All are wonderful when He stands revealed to the soul in any of His roles.

The soul needs such an acquaintance with Him that will excite and constantly keep awake its wonder and adoration. Contemplate Christ from any point of view, and the wonder of the soul is excited. Look at any feature of His character, at any portion of the plan of salvation, at any part that He takes in the glorious work of man's redemption—look steadfastly at Him as He is revealed through the Gospel by the Holy Spirit at any time and place, in any of His works or ways—and the soul will instantly exclaim, "Wonderful!" Yes, He *will be called Wonderful* (Isaiah 9:6)!

Counselor

"His name will be called…Counselor" (v. 6). Who has made Jesus his wisdom and has not often recognized the appropriateness of calling Him Counselor? Until He is known and embraced in this role, it is not natural or possible for the soul to go to Him with implicit confidence in every case of doubt.

Almost everybody holds in theory the propriety and necessity of consulting Christ about the affairs that concern us and His church. But it is one thing to hold this opinion and quite another to spiritually see and embrace Christ as our Counselor. When this happens, then we will naturally call Him Counselor when approaching Him in secret. Then we will naturally turn to and consult Him on all occasions about everything that concerns us. Then we will consult Him with implicit confidence in His ability and willingness to give us the direction we need.

Thoroughly and spiritually knowing Christ as the Counselor is undoubtedly a condition of abiding steadfastly in Him. Unless the soul knows and appreciates its dependence on Him as Counselor, and unless it renounces its own wisdom and substitutes His wisdom for it by laying hold of Christ by faith, it will not continue to walk in His counsel. Consequently, it will not abide in His love.

The Mighty God

"His name will be called...Mighty God" (Isaiah 9:6). *"My Lord and my God!"* (John 20:28), exclaimed Thomas when Christ stood spiritually revealed to him. It was not merely what Christ said to Thomas on that occasion that caused him to utter this exclamation. Thomas indeed saw that Christ had been raised from the dead, but Lazarus had also been raised from the dead. The mere fact, therefore, that Christ stood before him as one raised from the dead could not have been proof that He was God. No doubt, the Holy Spirit

disclosed to Thomas at that moment the true divinity of Christ, just as believers in all ages have had Him spiritually revealed to them as the Mighty God.

I have long been convinced that it is useless, as far as any spiritual benefit is concerned, to attempt to convince Unitarians of the divinity of Christ.* The Scriptures are as plain as they can be on this subject, yet it is true that *"no one can say that Jesus is Lord except by the Holy Spirit"* (1 Corinthians 12:3). As I have often said, the Holy Spirit must personally reveal Christ to the inward man before He can be known as the mighty God.

What is Christ to someone who does not know Him as God? To such a soul, He cannot be a Savior. It is impossible for the soul to intelligently and without idolatry commit itself to Him as a Savior unless it knows Him to be the true God. It cannot innocently pray to Him or worship Him or commit itself to His keeping until it knows Him as the mighty God.

To be orthodox merely in theory and in opinion is nothing in the matter of salvation. The soul must *know* Christ as God—must believe in or receive Him as such. To receive Him as anything

---

* A Unitarian is one who denies the doctrine of the Trinity and ascribes divinity to God the Father only.

else is an entirely different thing than coming and submitting to Him as the true, living, and mighty God.

Our Shield

Christ is our Shield. By this name or in this role He has always been known to believers. God said to Abraham, *"I am your shield"* (Genesis 15:1). The Scriptures also tell us, *"He is...our shield"* (Psalm 33:20), and, *"He is a shield to those who put their trust in Him"* (Proverbs 30:5).

A shield is a piece of defensive armor used in war. It is a broad plate made of wood or metal, worn on the arm and hand, and placed between the body and the enemy to protect it against his arrows or his blows. God is the Christian's shield in spiritual warfare. This is a most interesting and important role. The person who does not know Christ in this role, the one who has not embraced Him and put Him on as one would buckle on a shield, is completely exposed to the assaults of the Enemy and will surely be wounded, if not slain, by his fiery darts.

Christ as our Shield is more than a figure of speech. No fact or reality is of greater importance to the Christian than to know how to hide himself behind and in Christ in the hour of conflict. Unless the Christian has on his Shield and knows how to use it, he will surely fall in battle. When

Satan appears, the soul must present its Shield, must take refuge behind and in Christ, or all will be defeat and disgrace. When faith presents Christ as the Shield, Satan always leaves the field defeated.

Christ always makes a way for our escape (1 Corinthians 10:13), and never has a believer been wounded in conflict if he has properly used the Shield. But Christ needs to be known as our protection, as ready on all occasions to shield us from the curse of the law and from the artillery of the enemy of our souls. Be sure to truly know Him and put Him on as your Shield, and then you will always sing of victory.

Our Portion

The Lord is the Portion of His people. *"I am...your exceedingly great reward"* (Genesis 15:1), said God to Abraham. If we are to abide in Christ, we need to know and embrace Him as the Reward or Portion of the soul. We need to know Him as our *"exceedingly great reward,"* a present, all-satisfying portion.

Unless we know Christ so that we are satisfied with Him as all we can ask for or desire, we will not, of course, abstain from all forbidden sources of enjoyment. Nothing is more indispensable to our entire sanctification than to understand the fullness there is in Christ as our Portion. When the soul finds all its desires and all its needs fully met in Him, when it sees in Him all that it can conceive of as excellent and desirable, it remains at rest. There is little temptation to go after other gods or after other sources of enjoyment. The soul is full. It has enough. It has an infinitely rich and glorious inheritance. What more can it ask or think?

The soul that understands what it means to have Christ as its portion knows that He is an infinite portion. Eternity can never exhaust or even diminish our Portion in the least degree. For all eternity, the mind will increase in its capacity and enjoyment. Nothing can diminish any part of the infinite fullness of the divine Portion of our souls.

Our Hope

Christ is also our Hope: *"Paul, an apostle of Jesus Christ, by the commandment of God our Savior and the Lord Jesus Christ, our hope"* (1 Timothy 1:1). *"To them God willed to make known what are the riches of the glory of this mystery among the Gentiles: which is Christ in you, the hope of glory"* (Colossians 1:27).

Our only rational expectation is from Him. Christ in us is our *"hope of glory."* Without Christ in us, we have no well-grounded hope of glory. Christ in the Gospel, Christ on the cross, Christ risen, or Christ in heaven is not our hope; but Christ in us, Christ actually present, living, and reigning in us as truly as He lives and reigns in glory, is our only well-grounded Hope. We must be certain of this, for unless we despair of finding salvation in ourselves or in any other source, we do not truly make Christ our Hope.

The person who does not spiritually know Christ in this role has no well-grounded hope. He may hope that he is a Christian. He may hope that his sins are forgiven—that he will be saved. But he can have no good hope of glory. He must absolutely despair of obtaining help and salvation in any way except by Christ in him before he can know and embrace Christ as his Hope. This cannot be too fully understood or too deeply realized.

Many seem to think of Christ as their Hope only in His outward role, that is, as an atoning Savior, as a risen and ascended Savior. But the indispensable necessity of having Christ within them ruling in their hearts and establishing His government over their whole beings is a condition of salvation that they have not thought of. Christ cannot truly be our saving hope any further than He is received into and reigns in our souls. To hope in merely an outward Christ is to hope in vain.

To hope in Christ with a true Christian hope implies the following:

1. The ripe and spiritual understanding of our hopeless condition without Him

2. An understanding of our sins that will annihilate all hope of salvation on the ground of obeying the law

3. A perception of our spiritual bondage to sin that will annihilate all hope of salvation without His constant influence and strength to keep us from sin

4. A knowledge of our circumstances of temptation that will empty us of all expectation of fighting our own battles or of making the least degree of headway against our spiritual foes in our own wisdom and strength

5. A complete annihilation of all hope from any source other than Christ

Our Salvation

Christ is also our Salvation. Many Scriptures attest to this fact:

The LORD is my strength and song, and He has become my salvation; He is my God, and I will praise Him; my father's God, and I will exalt Him. (Exodus 15:2)

The LORD is my light and my salvation; whom shall I fear? The LORD is the strength of my life; of whom shall I be afraid? (Psalm 27:1)

Make haste to help me, O Lord, my salvation! (Psalm 38:22)

In God is my salvation and my glory; the rock of my strength, and my refuge, is in God. (Psalm 62:7)

Behold, God is my salvation, I will trust and not be afraid; "for YAH, the LORD ["the LORD JEHOVAH" KJV], is my strength and song; He also has become my salvation." (Isaiah 12:2)

For my eyes have seen Your salvation. (Luke 2:30)

Indeed He says, "It is too small a thing that You should be My Servant to raise up the tribes of Jacob, and to restore the preserved ones of Israel; I will also give You as a light to the Gentiles, that You should be My salvation to the ends of the earth." (Isaiah 49:6)

These and multitudes of similar passages present Christ not only as our Savior, but as our Salvation. That is, He saves us by becoming our Salvation. Becoming our Salvation includes and implies the following things:

1. Atoning for our sins

2. Convicting us of and converting us from our sins

3. Sanctifying our souls

4. Justifying or pardoning us and receiving us to favor

5. Giving us eternal life and happiness

6. Bestowing Himself upon us as the Portion of our souls

7. Uniting our souls with Him for eternity

Christ does all this for us. He may well be regarded not only as our Savior, but as our Salvation.

The Rock of Our Salvation

Christ is also the Rock of our Salvation, as the following verses show us:

He shall cry to Me, "You are my Father, my God, and the rock of my salvation." (Psalm 89:26)

But the LORD has been my defense, and my God the rock of my refuge. (Psalm 94:22)

Oh come, let us sing to the LORD! Let us shout joyfully to the Rock of our salvation. (Psalm 95:1)

*You have forgotten the God of your salvation,
and have not been mindful of the Rock of your
stronghold.* (Isaiah 17:10)

*A man will be as a hiding place from the wind,
and a cover from the tempest, as rivers of water
in a dry place, as the shadow of a great rock in
a weary land.* (Isaiah 32:2)

It is deeply interesting and very touching to
contemplate the roles in which Christ revealed
Himself to the Old Testament saints. He is the
Rock of our Salvation—a stronghold or place of
refuge. The soul must know Him in this role and
must take hold of Him and take shelter in Him.

A Cleft Rock

He is also the Cleft Rock from which the
waters of life flow. *"And all drank the same spiritual drink. For they drank of that spiritual Rock
that followed them, and that Rock was Christ"* (1
Corinthians 10:4). As such, the soul must know
and embrace Him.

A Great Rock

He is the Great Rock that is higher than we
are. Our Rock rises amid the burning sands of
our pilgrimage, and under its cooling shadow
our souls can find rest and comfort. He is like

"the shadow of a great rock in a weary land" (Isaiah 32:2).

To understand Christ in this role, the soul needs to be brought into sharp and extended trials until it is faint and ready to sink in discouragement, until the struggle is too severe for longer endurance and the soul is at the point of giving up in despair. Then, when Christ is revealed as our Great Rock standing for the soul's defense against the heat of its trials, throwing over it the cooling, soothing influence of His protection, the soul finds itself refreshed and at rest. Then the soul readily adopts the language of many passages of Scripture, and it understands Christ as inspired men understood and embraced Him.

It is truly remarkable that, in all our experiences, we can find that the inspired writers had similar experiences. In every trial and in every deliverance, in every new discovery of our emptiness and of Christ's fullness, we find the language of the living oracles. We readily discover that inspired men fell into similar trials and had Christ revealed to them in the same roles. This is so true that no language of our own can so readily express all that we think and feel and see.

The Rock That Gives Honey

He is the Rock from which the soul is satisfied with honey. *"He would have fed them also with the finest of wheat; and with honey from the rock I would have satisfied you*" (Psalm 81:16). The spiritual mind understands this language spiritually, as it is undoubtedly intended to be understood. The divine sweetness that often refreshes the spiritual mind when it goes to Christ reminds it of the words of this passage of Scripture. It knows what it means to be satisfied with honey from the Rock.

The Foundation of the Church

He is the Rock or Foundation upon which the church as the temple of the living God is built: *"On this rock I will build My church, and the gates of Hades shall not prevail against it"* (Matthew 16:18). *"'The stone which the builders rejected has become the chief cornerstone,' and 'A stone of stumbling and a rock of offense.' They stumble, being disobedient to the word, to which they also were appointed"* (1 Peter 2:7–8). *"As it is written: 'Behold, I lay in Zion a stumbling stone and rock of offense, and whoever believes on Him will not be put to shame'"* (Romans 9:33).

He is our sure Foundation. He is an eternal rock, or the Rock of Ages—the Cornerstone of the whole spiritual edifice. But we must build for ourselves upon this Rock. It is not enough to understand as a tenet, a theory, an opinion, an article of our creed, that Christ is the Rock in this sense. We must see to it that we do not build on the sand, but rather, on Him.

But everyone who hears these sayings of Mine, and does not do them, will be like a foolish man who built his house on the sand: and the rain descended, the floods came, and the winds blew and beat on that house; and it fell. And great was its fall. (Matthew 7:26–27)

The Strength of Our Hearts

He is the Strength of Our Hearts. He is not only our strength in conflicts with outward temptations, as expressed in Psalm 46:1: *"God is our refuge and strength, a very present help in trouble,"* but He is also the Strength of Our Hearts, as expressed in Psalm 73:26: *"My flesh and my heart fail; but God is the strength of my heart and my portion forever."* He strengthens the whole inner man in the way of holiness.

What Christian has not at times found himself ready to falter and faint along the way? Temptation seems to come unexpectedly upon him. He finds his spiritual strength very low and his resolution weak, and he feels as if he will give way to the slightest temptation. He is afraid to venture out of his room, or even to remain in it, lest he should sin. He says with David, *"I shall perish…by the hand of Saul"* (1 Samuel 27:1). He finds himself empty—all weakness and trembling.

If it were not for Christ—the Strength of His Heart—intervening just in time, he would undoubtedly experience his worst fears. But what believer in Christ has not often experienced His faithfulness under such circumstances and felt an immortal awaking, reviving, and strength taking possession of his whole being?

What minister has not often dragged himself into the pulpit so discouraged and faint that he is hardly able to stand or to hold up his head? He is so weak that his spiritual knees knock together. He is truly empty and feels as if he could not open his mouth. He sees himself as a barren vine, an empty vessel, a poor, helpless, strengthless infant lying in the dust before the Lord, unable to stand, go, preach, pray, or do the least thing for Christ.

But behold! At this juncture, his spiritual strength is renewed. Christ—the Strength of His Heart—develops His own almightiness within him. The minister's mouth is opened. He is *strong in faith, giving glory to God*" (Romans 4:20 KJV). At once he is made a sharp threshing instrument to beat down the mountains of opposition to Christ and His Gospel (Isaiah 41:15). Christ opens his mouth and fills it with arguments. Christ dresses him for battle. *"His bow remain*[s] *in strength, and the arms of his hands* [are] *made strong by the hands of the Mighty God of Jacob"* (Genesis 49:24).

The same is true of every Christian. He has his seasons of being empty so that he may feel his dependence. However, soon he is clothed with strength from on high, and an immortal, superhuman strength takes possession of his soul. The enemy gives way before him. In Christ he can run against a troop, and in His strength he can leap over a wall (2 Samuel 22:30). Every difficulty gives way before him, and he is conscious that Christ has fortified him with strength in his soul. The will seems to have the utmost decision, so that temptation gets an emphatic "no" without a moment's hesitation.

The One through Whom We Are Dead to Sin and Alive to God

Christ is the One through whom we may count ourselves *"dead indeed to sin, but alive to God"* (Romans 6:11). We are exhorted and commanded to do this. That is, through Him we may and ought to consider ourselves dead to sin and alive to God. But what is implied in this liberty to count ourselves dead to sin and alive to God through Jesus Christ our Lord? Why, certainly all of the following:

1. Through and in Him we have all the provision we need to keep us from sin.

2. We may and ought to expect to live without sin.

3. We ought to consider ourselves as having nothing more to do with sin than a dead man has to do with the affairs of this world.

4. We may and ought to take hold of Christ for this full and present death to sin and life to God.

5. If we do consider ourselves dead to sin and alive to God in the true spiritual sense of this text, we will find Christ to be to our souls all we expect of Him in this role.

If Christ cannot or will not save us from sin, on the condition of our taking hold of Him and considering ourselves dead to sin and alive to God through Him, what right did the apostle Paul have to say, *"Reckon yourselves to be dead indeed to sin, but alive to God in Christ Jesus our Lord"* (Romans 6:11)? What! When the apostle told us to consider ourselves dead to sin, will theologians tell us that such an expectation is a dangerous delusion?

Now, what does it mean to consider ourselves dead to sin and alive to God through Jesus Christ? Certainly nothing less than that, through Christ, we should expect to live without sin. Not to expect to live without sin through Christ is unbelief. It is a rejection of Christ in this role.

Through Christ we ought to expect to be alive to God as much as we expect to live at all. He who does not expect this rejects Christ as his Sanctification. He rejects Him as Jesus, the One who saves His people from their sins (Matthew 1:21).

Conclusion

In my estimation, the members of the church, I mean the nominal church, have entirely mistaken the nature and means of sanctification. They have not regarded it as entire consecration, nor have they understood that continual entire consecration is entire sanctification. They have regarded sanctification as the annihilation of the inborn tendencies instead of the controlling of them.

They are equally wrong about the means of entire sanctification. They seem to think that sanctification is brought about by a physical cleansing in which man is passive. Or they seem to go to the other extreme and think that sanctification is brought about by forming habits of obedience.

There are two schools of thought on sanctification. The old school seem to be waiting for a physical sanctification in which they are to be mostly passive. Furthermore, they do not even expect this sanctification to take place in this life. Since they believe that the constitution, or makeup, of both soul and body is defiled or sinful in every power and faculty, they, of course, cannot believe in entire sanctification in this life. If the constitutional appetites, passions, and tendencies are, in fact, as they believe, sinful in themselves, why, the question is then settled: entire sanctification cannot take place in this world or in the next, except as the makeup is radically changed by the creative power of God.

The new school, rejecting the doctrine of constitutional moral depravity and physical regeneration and sanctification, and also losing sight of Christ as our Sanctification, have fallen into a self-righteous view of sanctification. They believe that sanctification is brought about by works, by forming holy habits and so on. Both the old and the new school have fallen into glaring errors on this fundamentally important subject.

The truth beyond all question is that sanctification is by faith and not works. That is, faith receives Christ to the soul in all His offices and in all the fullness of His roles. When Christ is received, He works in the soul to will and to do all of His good pleasure (Philippians 2:13), not by a physical working, but by a moral or persuasive working. Observe that He influences the will. This must be by a moral influence, if the soul's actions are intelligent and free, as they must be to be holy. That is, if God influences the will to obey

Him, it must be by a divine moral persuasion. The soul never obeys in a spiritual and true sense unless it is influenced by the indwelling Spirit of Christ.

Whenever Christ is understood and received in any role, in that role He is full and perfect, so that we are *"complete in Him"* (Colossians 2:10). *"For it pleased the Father that in Him all the fullness should dwell"* (Colossians 1:19). And it pleased God that we might all receive of His fullness (John 1:16) until we have grown up into Him in all things (Ephesians 4:15), *"till we all come to the unity of the faith and of the knowledge of the Son of God, to a perfect man, to the measure of the stature of the fullness of Christ"* (v. 13).

Index to the Roles of Christ

About the Author

◇◆◇

Charles G. Finney (1792–1875) was a man with a message that burned through the religious deadwood and secular darkness of his time. He had the ability to shock both saint and sinner alike. Because he was radical in both his methods and his message, Finney was criticized for almost everything except being boring.

Born in Connecticut in 1792, Finney was nearly thirty years of age before he turned from his skepticism regarding Christianity and whole-heartedly embraced the Bible as the true Word of God. He gave up his law profession in order to spread the Gospel, and he soon became the most noteworthy revivalist of the nineteenth century, one of the leaders of the Second Great Awakening. It is estimated that over 250,000 souls were converted as a result of his preaching.

In 1832, Finney began pastoring Second Free Presbyterian Church in New York City.

In 1835, upon the request of Arthur Tappan, Finney established the theology department at Oberlin Collegiate Institute (today known as Oberlin College). He served there as a professor of theology as well as pastor of Oberlin's First Congregational Church until a few years before his death. He was also a member of the Oberlin College Board of Trustees from 1846 until he was elected president in 1851. During these years, he continued to carry on his evangelism, even visiting Great Britain twice in 1849–50 and 1859–60.

Finney was married three times in his life, first to Lydia Root Andrews (m. 1824), then to Elizabeth Ford Atkinson (m. 1848), and then to Rebecca Allen Rayl (m. 1865). All three of these women assisted Finney in his evangelistic efforts, accompanying him on his revival tours during their lives. In August of 1875, Finney died in Oberlin following a heart ailment.

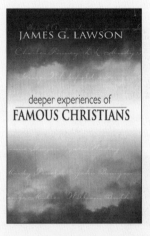